# Amazing Secrets of Human Sexuality Revealed

The ancient Taoists brought human sexuality to a higher level than any other group. Now their secrets can be yours. *The Tao and the Tree of Life* describes the entire structure of Taoist Internal Alchemy by comparing it with the Hebrew and Western traditions of Kaballah. Explore techniques that go far beyond anything previously published.

Basic concepts as well as some of the highest esoteric formulas of Taoist Internal Alchemy are explained in a clear and practical manner—much of this material has never before been available. Get started right away with simple exercises, suitable for the beginner or the advanced student, and improve your life immediately. The practices of Taoist Internal Alchemy are made accessible once and for all.

Learn the alchemical and sexual secrets long hidden within the *Zohar* and *Sepher Yetzirah*. Uncover the techniques of Taoist Internal Alchemy and experience the wisdom and power of *The Tao and the Tree of Life*.

# About the Author

Eric Steven Yudelove has been a student, practitioner, and teacher of the Kaballah, the Western Magical tradition, shamanism, the *I Ching*, and Taoist Internal Alchemy and Chi Kung since 1970. He was one of the first American students to study with the renowned Tao master Mantak Chia. He has studied with Kabbalists of both the Hebrew and Western tradition and was initiated as a shaman in 1984.

Eric, a licensed professional and businessman, resides with his wife, four children, and dog in a suburb of New York City.

# To Write the Author

If you wish to contact the author or would like more information about this book, please write to the author in care of Llewellyn Worldwide, and we will forward your request. Both the author and publisher appreciate hearing from you and learning of your enjoyment of this book and how it has helped you. Llewellyn Worldwide cannot guarantee that every letter written to the author can be answered, but all will be forwarded. Please write to:

Eric Yudelove
c/o Llewellyn Worldwide
P.O. Box 64383, Dept. K250-X,
St. Paul, MN 55164-0383, U.S.A.

Please enclose a self-addressed, stamped envelope for reply
or $1.00 to cover costs.If outside the U.S.A., enclose international
postal reply coupon.

# The Tao & The Tree of Life

## Alchemical & Sexual Mysteries of the East and West

## Eric Yudelove

1996
Llewellyn Publications
St. Paul, Minnesota 55164-0383

FIRST EDITION
Second Printing, 1996

Cover design by Tom Grewe
Interior layout and design by Laura Gudbaur
Editing by Laura Gudbaur and Darwin Holmstrom
Interior illustrations redrawn with permission from illustrations originally drawn by Juan Li, Mantak Chia and Maneewan Chia for Healing Tao Press

Library of Congress Cataloging-In-Publication Data
Yudelove, Eric, 1946-
        The tao & the tree of life: alchemical & sexual mysteries of the East and West / by Eric Yudelove.
                p. cm. -- (Llewellyn's world magic series)
        Includes bibliographical references (p. ) and index.
    ISBN 1-56718-250-X (trade pbk.)
    1. Magic. 2. Tao--Miscellanea. 3. Cabala. 4. Yoga. 5. Shaman-ism. 6. Alchemy. 7. Sex--Miscellanea. I. Title. II. Series.
    BF1621.Y83  1996                              95-47291
    299'.93--dc20                                 CIP

Llewellyn Publications
A Division of Llewellyn Worldwide, Ltd.
P.O. Box 64383-0383
St. Paul, Minnesota 55164-0383

# Llewellyn's World Religion & Magic Series

There is an almost magical quality that lies at the core of every religion and mystical system.

Through this we see the world as alive, as the home which humanity shares with forces and powers both visible and invisible, with which we can interface to either our advantage or disadvantage—depending upon our awareness and intention.

We can tap into this quality as a way of seeing and relating to the creative powers, the living energies, the all-pervading spirit, the underlying intelligence that is the universe within which we and all else exist. All share the same goals and the same limitations: always seeking truth, forever haunted by human limitations in perceiving that truth. Finding the common elements in different approaches can broaden our understanding of all systems.

The study of the world's mystical systems not only enhances your understanding of the world in which you live, and hence your ability to live better, but brings you in touch with the inner essence of your long evolutionary heritage and most particularly with the archetypal images and forces most alive in your whole consciousness.

# Table of Contents

# *Foreword*

I have spent most of my life studying and teaching the Tao. It has been my privilege to bring these long-time secret teachings to many thousands of students all over the world. And in July of 1994, a dream came true for me when a permanent Taoist center was opened at Tao Garden in Chiang Mai, Thailand. Students from any corner of the globe can come and study, spend some time, or even live here.

From late 1977 until July 1994, I lived in and around New York City. This was my base to bring the teachings of the Healing Tao to the Western World. It was a great adventure for me and my wife, Maneewan, to leave Thailand and come to New York. When we first arrived in America, there was no one else teaching the esoteric yoga of the Taoists. Only a few Chinese doctors recognized what I was teaching. And for the first few years, almost all my students were Chinese.

The main exception was my very first American student who turned out to be my immigration lawyer. I had listed my occupation as Internal Needleless Accupuncture on an interview card. At our first meeting, he started questioning me about it. I explained that I could pass healing energy through my hands and transmit it to another person. But, that this was only a small part of what I hoped to teach in America. I told him that I had developed and organized a system that I then called Taoist esoteric yoga. I had studied with numerous Masters all over the Orient. After many years at this, I realized that there were so many different practices that it would take me lifetimes to learn them all. I was already proficient in Chinese, Indian, Tibetan and Japanese methods. For me they all fit together as part of the Tao. And this is what I would teach.

I had first started studying meditation when I was six years old. My family was Christian, but in Thailand, where I grew up, there were so many Buddhist temples near my house. On weekends and holidays I would often visit the temples. During summer vacation, I stayed with the monks for weeks and learned the meditation of sitting and stilling the mind.

As a youth, I studied Thai boxing, *aikido, tai chi* and yoga. I was then sent to school in Hong Kong and it was there that I met Master Yi-Eng (One Cloud) when I was 16 and he initiated me into Taoist esoteric practices. It was his senior student, Cheng Sue Sue, who three years later taught me to open the Microcosmic Orbit and later on I learned the many formulas of Taoist Internal Alchemy from Master Yi-Eng.

After this, I sought out and studied with many other masters and learned numerous forms of Chi Kung (Chinese breath and movement exercises), Kung Fu, and Taoist Sexual Yoga. Eventually, I became a Master and established myself in Bangkok. It was my first Master, Yi-Eng, who encouraged me and gave me permission to come to America and teach the long-secret Taoist practices.

As I related my story to my immigration lawyer, he informed me that he was an adept of a Western esoteric system known as the Kabbalah. Now, I had heard of the Kabbalah but I knew nothing about it. I had never met a Kabbalist in the Orient. He was fascinated by what I told him and, for a time, he became a devoted student, actually living with me and Maneewan in our first apartment in Brooklyn. It was in this manner that I learned about the Kabbalah. At the time, I only learned the most basic theory. I was most concerned with teaching the Tao. But I realized that there were many similarities between the Taoist and Kabbalistic practices.

By late 1981, my English had improved to the point that I decided to seek a wider English-speaking audience. I had written and privately printed an early edition of my first book *Awaken Healing Energy Through the Tao*, and had opened the Taoist Esoteric Yoga Center at Confucius Plaza in Chinatown, New York.

On December 4th and 5th, 1981, I held my first regularly scheduled seminar on the Microcosmic Orbit. Many of the students who came to that first seminar have stayed with me and continued to study and practice and become teachers themselves. That small group included Michael Winn, Ron Diana, Sharon Smith, Raven Merle (now Cohen) and Eric Yudelove. They were an enthusiastic bunch and eagerly gobbled up each new course I taught. By March of 1982, they had also learned Fusion of the Five Elements, Seminal Kung Fu and Iron Shirt Chi Kung. That summer, we held our first retreat in Andover, Massachusetts. It was a wonderful week filled with Taoist practices that had never been seen before in the West.

I had begun holding teacher training sessions at my house for my most serious students. In 1983, a small group of these students became the first teachers of the Healing Tao. Eric was one of them.

Over the years, Eric has remained a faithful student, practitioner and friend. His ability to absorb and understand Taoist Internal Alchemy is evident in this book. He had me read and approve the sections dealing with the Taoist practices. For much of the time that I lived in the New York area, I made my home in the town of Huntington. Eric lived just a few minutes away. We learned a lot from each other. Eric had a vast knowledge of the Kabbalah. We often discussed the similarities and differences between Taoist Yoga and the Kabbalah. It was from him that I learned that there are actually two Kabbalahs: one strictly Jewish and the other derived from the Western esoteric tradition. My immigration lawyer was a Western Kabbalist. Eric is well-versed in both forms.

There was always a sense of mystery and magic around Eric. As a teacher of the Tao, I have the opportunity to meet many unique individuals. He is a true blend of the rational and the mystic. What you read in this book is based on his own experiences. It is not just theory. Because we lived so close to each other, I was able to teach Eric the very highest formulas of Taoist Internal Alchemy. But often, through his own practice, he would come to me and tell me what he was experiencing and I would realize that he had arrived at a higher formula on his own.

Eric also knows many different esoteric systems. He was the first to teach me the shamanic practice of journeying into the Earth to meet power animals and plants. I suspect that he has an immortal spirit guide. But with all this, he still remains rooted in the everyday world. He is a good family man. His oldest son is the same age as my son, Max. And, like the first

Kabbalist I met, he, too, is a skilled lawyer who has often helped me professionally.

I encouraged Eric to write this book. In it he has opened up new pathways between the East and the West. The Tao is great beyond comprehension and contains all things. Kabbalah is one form of Western man's dealing with the Tao. It is all part of the One. Here, for the first time, we have an opportunity to compare these wondrous systems, Taoist Alchemy and the Kabbalah.

I tell you that I like some of the Kabbalah practices. Especially the Lightning Flash. It is a good way to move the *Chi* energy quickly through the body.

In Taoist Internal Alchemy, it is so important to learn to direct the energy inside of you with your mind. The mind guides the *Chi* through the meridians and into the internal organs, connective tissue and bones as well. What is important is to gain control of the flow of *Chi*.

The Taoists have many methods to learn to control the *Chi*. In Internal Alchemy we learn how to guide the *Chi* and also how to build it up. We use sexual energy to strengthen the *Chi*. We use breath to fan the *Chi* and strengthen the flow of Primordial Energy.

The *Chi* of the body is then harmonized and built up again. Then it is transformed into a new form of *Chi*, powered by your own sexual energy which we call *Jing*.

The various transformations lead to the creation of a new entity within you. This entity, this little pearl, is the immortal part of you. You have created something where before there was nothing. This immortal part comes to realize its oneness with the immortal universe.

I tell you that Eric's description of Taoist Alchemy is so clear. In none of my own books do I have such a detailed look at the entire system, from basic practices such as the Inner Smile and the Six Healing Sounds, to the most advanced alchemical formulas. So, he does Taoists a service all over the world in carrying on my own mission which is to teach the Healing Tao.

Eric was already a Kabbalist when I first met him almost fifteen years ago. He was always interested in similarities between the practices of Kabbalah and Taoist Alchemy. But, I tell you Kabbalah is so complicated. I'll let Eric explain it to you. But the two systems are very similar. We should learn from each other.

So, I want to say that I hope Eric comes to Thailand and that the publication of this book, *The Tao & the Tree of Life*, starts a whole new adventure in his life.

Master Mantak Chia
Tao Garden
Chiang Mai, Thailand
March 7, 1995

# *Introduction*

Life is an adventure. We never know in advance what unexpected twists and turns it can take. Where will life take us?

Will it give us happiness and success, or misery and boredom? Will we reach the heights or the depths, or just hang out somewhere in between?

My life has thankfully been more interesting than I would have ever imagined. I attribute this to a natural mystical inclination, good genes, surprising determination in the face of adversity, a great wife and a most unusual fate decreed by powers far greater then myself. I'm also quite curious and analytical by nature.

It should come as no surprise that I would spend a good part of my life exploring various esoteric traditions and arcane sciences. It just happened naturally. Every time I tried to get away from the mystical, it drew me back one way or another. Finally, after years of struggling against its unerring pull, I just gave up the struggle and accepted this side of myself as part of my true nature. During all these years I balanced out my life by working as a professional, always able to support myself, my wife, and my children. Somehow it all worked out. There were ups and downs, leaps into the void with eyes closed, successes and failures and unexpected moments of pleasure.

This book is a bit of a summary of my investigations into esoteric traditions. Surely Taoist Internal Alchemy and the Kabbalah are two of the most obscure traditions in existence. This probably explains their attraction to me.

The Taoists and the Kabbalists have much in common. This is not well known even to seekers of the mysteries. Both have suffered from persecution during their long histories. In the past fifty years alone, both the Jews who gave birth to the Kabbalah, and the Taoists were almost exterminated from the face of the Earth.

The Taoists have suffered a harsh fate in their native China since the Communist Revolution. They were killed and hounded, forced to live their lives in shame and under house arrest. By 1973, author John Blofeld, writing in *Taoist Mysteries and Magic*, actually feared that the true Taoist tradition had perished. Luckily, a few Tao masters escaped to Thailand, Hong Kong, Taiwan, and other parts of the Orient. As I understand the current situation, there are virtually no Tao Masters left in China. The Chinese government now regrets this great loss and actually sponsors the revival of Taoist practices like *Tai Chi* and *Chi Kung* exercises, which have become a phenomenon in China.

During much of its history the Kabbalah survived in secrecy. It was often seen as a threat to the established religious orthodoxy. There were only a few times in its history that it existed out in the open, as part of mainstream Judaism. This is certainly not true today. Many Jews do not realize that

the Kabbalah fell into disfavor as a result of its close associa-
tion to the false Jewish Messiah Shabbatai Zevi in the seven-
teenth century. Zevi had convinced most of the Jewish world
that he was the fulfillment of messianic Kabbalistic prophecy.
When he was arrested by the Sultan of Constantinople and
given the choice to die or convert to Islam, poor Shabbatai
chose to convert. From then on the Kabbalah sunk into
obscurity. Most Jews have never heard of Shabbatai Zevi, his
memory was understandably suppressed, but they still shud-
der unknowingly when the word Kabbalah is mentioned.

There is also an offshoot of the Jewish Kabbalah known
variously as the Western Tradition, Christian Kabbalah or
Western Kabbalah. This one is even more obscure than Taoist
Internal Alchemy or the Hebrew Kabbalah. That's why I
really love it. They are all testament to man's quest for knowledge and understanding of the universe we live in. I began my
studies with the Western Tradition, the *I Ching*, and the Kabbalah. After many adventures and misadventures, my path led
me to alchemy. I'm referring to Western inner (spiritual)
alchemy and not outer alchemy (the physical process of
changing lead into gold). At first, I was stymied. I could
understand some of the concepts, but I had absolutely no idea
of what the methodology was.

The Western alchemical tradition was a closed door.
Through reading, I became aware of the Chinese inner
alchemical tradition. Supposedly, the aims were the same,
they just had different cultural backgrounds. Surprisingly, I
found Chinese inner alchemy much more accessible.

In the early 1970's, when I first began to read about this
Chinese alchemy, only one book about this subject was actu-
ally available. This was the great classic *The Secret of the Golden
Flower*, translated by Richard Wilhelm. This short book was

pure magic. Over a period of years, I read it and reread it. Slowly, its secrets began to unravel, like peeling the layers from an onion. Each time I read it, it seemed to be a different book.

Here was an ancient, apparently authentic process of inner alchemy.

This Chinese inner alchemy was also called Taoist Yoga, a most benign name for this most esoteric and sublime study. Aleister Crowley, the English magician and Kabbalist was most enamored with the ancient Tao Masters and their reputed supernatural powers. Although I have seen no evidence in his writings that he knew the true practices of Taoist Yoga, my early readings of the respect Crowley had for these Tao Masters (and he apparently didn't respect too many people) served to further increase my desire to learn more of this mysterious practice.

In time, I came to grasp the essentials of *The Secret of the Golden Flower*. By reading and rereading and practicing, I learned the secret of circulating energy in the body. The book hinted at a method of retention of sexual energy, but was anything but specific.

I saw numerous similarities to Western practices and I continued my study of both traditions until an incident occurred in my study one night in late 1981 that caused me to realize just how powerful the Taoist practices really were. It occurred about two months after I found and began practicing the methods of the second Chinese alchemical text to be published in English, *Taoist Yoga*, by Charles Luk.

I was seated on the floor of my study circulating energy within my body. This consisted of causing energy (or *chi*) to rise from the base of the spine, up to the top of the head, and then circulate downward through the front of my body to the sexual region then back up the spine. As I did this, I felt a warmth inside. However, quite suddenly it seemed as if a furnace ignited within me and I actually felt as if I were burning up. My study glowed with an orange-golden light and I truly feared for my life. I immediately stopped the circulation and felt myself continue growing hotter and hotter. After a few minutes of terror, the heat began to decrease and soon faded away.

Feeling lucky to be alive, I vowed never to try this again unless and until I found a true Tao Master. In New York in 1981, this seemed a pretty remote possibility. And yet, within a month, I was able to find, quite possibly, the only Tao Master in America who was teaching the secrets of Taoist Yoga to the public. It was on a flyer, on a telephone pole in Chinatown advertising Taoist Esoteric Yoga taught by Master Mantak Chia. On a December night, in a basement room in Chinatown, I met Master Chia for the first time. He had just recently arrived in America. As I listened to him speak with his heavy Chinese accent, there was no doubt that he was teaching exactly what I was looking for.

Since that time, I have continued to study with Master Chia. I also continued my other studies which included being initiated into an American Indian shamanic tradition. On occasion, I even taught Master Chia about shamanism and the western study of the elements called Hermetics. By 1988, my Western-Jewish roots began to gnaw at me and I began devoting more time to the Kabbalah.

During all my years of study and practice, I tried to synthesize and compare the various systems I had learned. Much has been written about Kabbalah, Magick, Shamanism and Taoist Yoga in the past decade. Still, nothing to my knowledge has been written comparing and analyzing these analogous systems. I hope to remove some of the mystery from their names.

And, thus, this short book. The world is full of magick and mystery. If we can get beyond the routine, perhaps we can catch a glimpse and realize that it's all a great magic show. The Way of the Tao. Perhaps this is your path.

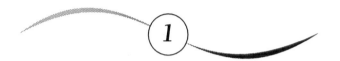

# The Shaman and the
# Three Worlds

The roots of all philosophy, religion, science, mysticism and magic go far back into the shroud of pre-history. Modern man, *homo sapiens*, is much older than most people realize. Recent findings in a cave in the Lower Galilee of Israel yielded bone fragments of what are believed to be modern man that are over 90,000 years old. If this is accurate, then it took thousands of years for our ancestors to push the older, more ape-like species, Neanderthal man, out of Europe and Asia. The wars must have raged on endlessly over thousands and thousands of years. In Europe and Asia, modern man leaves no known traces until between 35,000 and 40,000 years ago. These are men with brains and body structures like our own. They have left us a legacy of cave paintings but no written words. These paintings were often more than mere representations of people, animals, the hunt, or battle. They were magic tools used by the shaman to influence luck, prowess, health, fertility, etc., for his group or

1

tribe. The shaman or medicine man is the archetype of man as an intermediary between the visible and invisible worlds. He could commune with the spirits of nature, the spirits of plants and animals, protective forces, destructive forces, and various deities and spirit guides. To his community, the shaman was a healer, a magician, a priest, and a wise man.

The shamanic tradition is obviously ancient and developed over untold millennia. It followed prehistoric man as he spread his reach over the planet. Much has been written in this century about shamanism and, remarkably, the practices themselves, though they might be found on opposite ends of the earth, are basically consistent everywhere.

To ancient man, the inner world was just as real as the outer world. The shaman would journey into the inner world in order to influence the outer world. It is just this inner world journey that forms the basis for all meditative practices— Western Magick, the Kabbalah, Taoist Yoga, and all other inner-directed paths. In a certain sense, there is a tradition here that dates back perhaps more than 100,000 years, as old as *homo sapiens* himself.

How extraordinary, then, that man became aware of an inner world: a world of the mind, a world of dreams and visions. A world with its own laws and rules. How much more remarkable still that man could learn, in time, to manipulate this inner world, fill it with places to visit and things to see and beings to meet. This was a true evolutionary leap forward. Psychology would describe this as a descent into the unconscious in order to bring it to consciousness.

The first shamen were probably individuals with unusual abilities, such as a hunter who could apparently converse with the spirit of the lion, or a man who would have visions that always seemed to come true. These abilities would be recognized by the group and this special man gained a new status within it. Over generations, the abilities would be passed down or attempted to be passed down.

Eventually, certain traditions would arise. A dogma would be born and would continue until the tribe was conquered by another tribe with different shamanic traditions, or a shaman would have a new and more powerful vision that would overcome the old ways. Soon, there would be priests, some of whom were true shamen, and some of whom could only understand the dogma, but could not experience it on an inner level.

Thus, we have shamanism as the father and mother of both mysticism and religion; the esoteric and the exoteric; the secret and the known.

The shaman's universe consisted of three worlds—the Lower World, the Middle World, and the Upper World. We live in the Middle World, on the surface of the earth. The shaman could journey to either the Lower World, below the surface of the earth, or to the Upper World, above the earth according to his purpose.

In the Lower World, the shaman would find power animals and power plants and stones. In the Upper World, he would seek guidance from spirit guides and gods.

His means of travel was a meditational trance often propelled by rhythmic beating of drums or shaking of rattles. These would beat or shake at a set, constant pace and the shaman would use a meditational technique to begin his journey.

The Lower and Upper Worlds were vast domains that the shaman would learn to map out during his apprenticeship. All three worlds were equally real. One was not superior to the other. The Lower World was not inferior to the Upper World.

Neither was the Lower World any form of hell. It was a place to hunt for power just as the Upper World was a place to seek guidance.

## A Shamanic Journey

A journey to the Lower World begins with the shaman seated on the ground in the middle of a circle formed by members of his group, usually warriors or elders, as a number of large drums beat in unison. The shaman is seeking a power animal. The spirit of the power animal will animate the shaman's soul. It will give him the power necessary to be a shaman and work his seemingly miraculous ways. The shaman must travel down into the earth. In his mind, he goes to his special entrance into the ground. His is a small cave, a known entrance given to him as a shamanic gift by his teacher at the end of his apprenticeship.

The drums beat, in his mind the cave appears. He moves toward its opening. It is small and shaded. Once inside, the light disappears almost immediately as he begins to travel downward. He goes right through the earth; nothing stands in his way as he gains speed. The interior of the earth becomes visible as he continues downward like a projectile. He passes through a series of caverns, then arrives at a river that travels down like an endless waterslide. There is no fear, just a sense of anticipation. The river deposits him eventually on a rocky, forbidding shore. Around him are huge unscalable cliffs. He walks around; there is no way out. He's stuck. His shamanic senses tell him that this barrier has been placed here by a jealous rival. He must counteract the other shaman's magic. From his medicine pouch, he removes his magic stone which he has retrieved from the center of the earth on an earlier journey. He holds this stone in his open palm and it begins to glow and pulse. A beam of light shoots from the stone into the base of the dark cliff and an entrance way appears. He enters; the walls are covered with glowing crystals. He is safe; his power is still stronger than his rival. Soon, he begins a rapid descent through these crystal caves. Finally, the crystals disappear and he is in a long, dark tunnel. Far ahead is brilliant light. He walks toward it. It is the exit. Ahead is the lower world. He gets to the end of the tunnel and walks out into a sunlit plain covered with dense grass and groves of trees. He begins to hunt for his power animal, leaving the tunnel behind.

He moves out through the grass. In the distance, he hears the scream of an eagle. He begins to sing his power song, repeating it over and over like a chant. Soon, animals begin to appear. He sees two antelope grazing near a small watering hole. They look up at him and run away. A woolly rhino stamps across the plain off to the right, a saber-tooth tiger is flushed out of its lair and both disappear among the trees. These are not his animals.

The shaman continues to sing his song. He lifts up into the air and the landscape begins to shift below him. Soon, he arrives at a beach. Behind the sand is a large cave. A giant bear walks out onto the sand and moves toward the shaman. It is huge with cavernous jaws. The bear walks up to him, looking right into his eyes. It rears up on its hind legs and begins to circle the shaman as if it were dancing. After a complete circuit, the bear sits down on its haunches. The shaman moves closer. The bear embraces him with its great front paws.

The shaman has found his new power animal. He leaps on the bear's back with his arms around the enormous neck. He feels tremendous strength and power surging back and forth between him and the bear. The bear rises up on all four legs and begins to run across the sand with the shaman on his back singing his power song with new vigor and strength. The tempo increases. The shaman becomes aware of a rapid beating sound coming from far away. The drumming gets louder and faster. The drummers are calling him back from his journey.

The bear races off the beach and onto the plain. There ahead is the tunnel, the way back to the middle world. The shaman enters the tunnel at dizzying speed and begins to rise upward through the earth. He is aware of his bear's presence though he cannot see it. The journey upward is much more rapid than the descent. Soon, he is at the entrance way to his cave in the middle world. The drumming now comes in short staccato ripples. The journey is over. The shaman is back in the middle world.

He sits for a few minutes. Then, he slowly begins to chant his power song. He rises up on his legs and begins to dance. The power of the bear surges through him. He is dancing his power animal. The shaman dances his bear dance. The tribe looks on. They know that he has gained a new animal and great power. This year the hunting will be good.

During the life of a shaman, there may be many power animals. Often they come to the shaman, stay for a number of years and then leave. The shaman must then seek a new power animal in a fashion as set out above or risk losing his power. Usually, he has only one power animal at a time.

Power is a catch-all phrase to indicate the shaman's strength. He needs power to be strong in body and mind. Along with power, the shaman also journeys to the upper world to get guidance and advice from his spirit guides. This journey is similar to the journey to the lower world except the shaman travels upward to the place above the world.

In the Middle world, the "real world," the shaman makes use of his power and guidance. He can send out his power or fix it in a certain spot. He could imbue wall paintings with his power and thus energize them so that they are more than mere pictures. The shaman casts his spell, sends out his power so that the pictures become guarantees of success.

The shaman can use his power for healing by sending it into the patient's body to remove "evil influences."

## Taoist Yoga and the Kabbalah

Shamanism is the basis for all modern mystical and esoteric systems. In many parts of the world, it still exists in relatively pure form. I begin this book with a brief view of shamanism because it provides an excellent background for comparing Taoist Yoga and Kabbalistic theory and practice. Examined in terms of a Middle, Lower, and Upper world it becomes much easier to comprehend the methods and thinking of the Taoists and Kabbalists. (There is no standard spelling for Kabbalah, sometimes it is spelled Qabalah or Quabbalah. The spelling used here is the most familiar).

Taoist Yoga deals with all three of the worlds. Essentially, it is a very advanced shamanic system. The practice begins with strengthening the energy of the body, harmonizing this energy and increasing it. Then, this energy, or *chi*, is transformed into a new form of energy as the practitioner learns to draw energy from above and below while also gaining the ability to journey above or below.

The Kabbalah is more difficult to pin down because of the many different traditions. Among the strictly Jewish Kabbalists, it was expected that the Kabbalist would be married with children and be well versed in the law or Torah before learning the mysteries of Kabbalah. This law, by which the Jews were governed, relates to the Middle World. The Jewish Kabbalist would be most concerned with the Upper World. In later Jewish Kabbalism, the emphasis shifted somewhat to include the lower world, but in general, its aim was always above.

Western Kabbalism is much more shamanic in approach than its Jewish counterpart. Work is done in all three worlds.

Western Kabbalism is an esoteric system that seeks to induce transformations in the student's psyche as he or she seeks to accomplish the Great Work. In outlook, it is quite similar to Taoist Yoga. Accomplishing the Great Work is to a Western Kabbalist what obtaining the Secret of the Golden Flower is to a Taoist or obtaining Nirvana is to a Buddhist. It is arriving at the goal. Few seekers ever actually arrive, though many spend this life trying.

Western Kabbalism has yet to be legitimately accepted as a philosophy while Hebrew Kabbalism and Taoist Yoga are. A Jewish Kabbalist is often seen as a wise man, a practitioner of Taoist Yoga is mysterious but upright, a Western Kabbalist is often scoffed at or feared. This is unfortunate, but it is a prime reason why most of them work alone, or in groups, in secret. Another main reason is that Western Kabbalism has become synonymous with the name Magic, or as popularized by Aleister Crowley, Magick. In the West, there is no doubt that magic has a bad reputation. Yet, the word "Magus" does not conjure up this same dark image, although a Magus is surely a practitioner of magic. Magi is the plural form of magus. There's this story about these three Magi who followed a star ... you remember that story. Once upon a time, a Magus was considered to be a wise man. Yet, today magick is feared or laughed at. Did anyone ever think about what Magi do?

The beauty of Western Kabbalism is that it is very orderly and well constructed. It uses one basic diagram upon which the entire system can be laid out. This diagram is the Tree of Life. Everything in the universe, in this world, has a place on the Tree of Life. I will devote a later chapter to it. The Western Kabbalist or Magus does much of his work on the inner level. He learns to go up and down the Tree. Usually, his first initiation is into the earth. The general aim is upward though he always proclaims his aim is balance. The Magus builds an inner temple from which to travel. He always leaves from and returns to the earth. Thus, all three worlds—upper, middle and lower—are utilized.

The basic philosophy of the Magus is: the ultimate source of this universe is the Unknown. Therefore, everything in this universe is a manifestation from the Unknown. Both Hebrew Kabbalists and Taoist have this same basic belief.

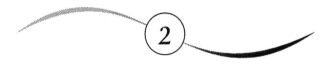

# The Missing Link: Jewish and Western Kabbalah

I n the beginning, the Kabbalah was strictly a Jewish system. It developed as an esoteric, or hidden, explanation of the meaning of the Torah.

The Torah is the first five books of the Bible. It is said to have been written by Moses and consists of the books Genesis, Exodus, Numbers, Leviticus, and Deuteronomy. It is handwritten on scrolls in synagogues all over the world and printed in Hebrew, English, French, Chinese, and so on, in every Bible published anywhere on earth.

It would appear obvious that mystical traditions would arise among the Jews, just as they did in all other religions.

The Kabbalah was a secret tradition for most of its history. It was an oral tradition handed down from master to disciple. The word *Kabbalah* translates "to receive," which is indicative of the apprentice relationship necessary to learn Kabbalah from a teacher.

## Early History of the Kabbalah

The early history of the Kabbalah is shrouded in mystery and legend. One legend tells that the Archangel Raziel taught Kabbalah to Adam after his expulsion from the Garden of Eden. Another attributes Abraham as the first Kabbalist and the author of the *Sepher Yetzirah,* one of the two classic texts of the Kabbalah. Another legend tells of Moses coming down from Mt. Sinai with the original Ten Commandments. On these original tablets were written the Kabbalah. When Moses saw the Jews worshipping the Golden Calf, he deemed them unworthy to receive this higher law and destroyed the original tablets. He then climbed to the heights of Mt. Sinai and returned to the people with a simple legal code to govern the rebellious, recently freed slaves of Pharaoh. The original ten rules of the Kabbalah were orally related to Aaron, the High Priest and Moses' brother. Thereafter, the Kabbalah was reserved for only the priesthood and the very learned. A man must first be learned in the law before he could approach the Kabbalah.

What makes the Jewish Kabbalah even more difficult is the fact that there were many different schools and systems. There is no one Kabbalah among the Jews. There is a body of knowledge that is composed of traditions arising during more than five thousand years of growth.

## The Tree of Life

During most of this time, the Kabbalah belonged exclusively to the Jews. In the twelfth century, the Kabbalah emerged from secrecy in Spain. It was here that the diagram known as the Tree of Life first appeared. This diagram is the missing link between the two traditions of Jewish and Western Kabbalism.

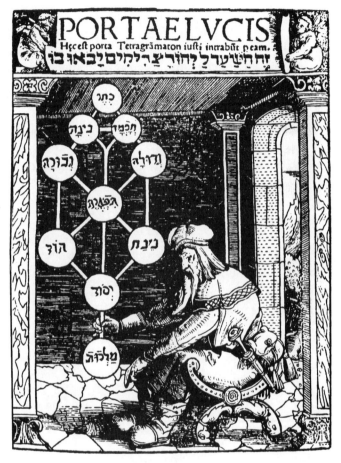

Figure 1: Bookplate from *Portae Lucis*, 1516

Almost all of Western Kabbalism is built upon this Tree. Jewish Kabbalism places much less emphasis upon it.

Specifically, its first appearance in a book was in *Portae Lucis* in 1516. This was a Latin translation of *Shaarei Orah (Gates of Light)* written by Rabbi Joseph Gikatalia (1248-1323) around the year 1290. This was a time of great messianic fervor among the Jews based on the prophetic teaching of Abraham Abulafia, the master Kabbalist. The book was not actually printed, though, until the year 1516 and existed until then in manuscript form. On the title page, a seated man is shown holding a tree with the ten sephiroth.

The publication of this book corresponds with the creation of a new Kabbalah. The term "Christian Kabbalah" could accurately be applied to this new Kabbalah at that point in time—1516. Strangely, a printed Hebrew version of this book did not appear until 1559. This was one year after the first printed edition of *The Zohar* appeared. *The Zohar* is a massive work. It is, along with the *Sepher Yetzirah*, the classic book of Jewish Kabbalism. It caused a revolutionary change in Jewish Kabbalah, but its influence barely touched Western Kabbalah.

However, this other little known book, *Portae Lucis*, exerted tremendous influence in two separate directions. Shortly after its publication in Latin, a group of fervent Dominicans tried to convince Pope Leo X to confiscate and burn all Jewish books. The Christian mystic, Johann Reuchlin (1455-1522), drew from this book in his own classic *De Arte Cabalistica (On the Art of the Kabbalah*, 1517) to convince the Pope, to whom it was dedicated, of the value of Jewish teachings and the Hebrew books were saved.

Reuchlin believed that the Kabbalah contained the doctrine of Christianity. He taught that in the age of the patriarchs, before Moses, God had a three lettered name such as YHV, the Trigramaton. Later in time, the four lettered name of God, the Tetragrammaton, YHVH, was first revealed to Moses, as stated in Exodus 3:15. In the Christian era, by adding the letter Shin to the Tetragrammaton you get the five letter name of god, the Pentagramaton, YHShVH. This is also the Hebrew spelling of Jesus' name. This was the early basis of Christian Kabbalah.

Reuchlin was also aware that the Kabbalists practiced their religion with devotional love of God rather than the more traditional fear of God. He thought that these Kabbalists were very "Christian" in their behavior. The Kabbalah also talked about the Messiah. Reuchlin tried to convince the Pope that the Kabbalists were really talking about Jesus. As a historical matter, the Kabbalists did not believe that the Messiah had yet appeared, while the Christians believed it was Jesus.

On the other hand, occult groups throughout Europe were greatly influenced by the teachings of this book. It continues to exert that influence today.

## Modern Jewish Kabbalah

The teachings in *Shaarei Orah* cannot be said to be at the heart of modern Jewish Kabbalah. As it exists today, most Jewish Kabbalists follow the teachings of *The Zohar* and its interpretations by the great Rabbi Isaac Luria (1524-1572) known as the *Ari*. Lurianic Kabbalism is vastly complex. However, its basic theory, when stripped down to essentials, is remarkably consistent with modern physics in describing the creation of the universe and its evolution.

It is Lurianic Kabbalism that expanded the importance of the Lower World in Jewish Kabbalism. This Lower World is a dark, demonic place where sparks of divine light live in exile. The Lurianic Kabbalist uses a meditational technique to travel to the Lower World (the world of the Qlippoth) to rescue the divine sparks and bring them to the Upper World. This was called a Unification because God's exiled light was being brought together with its source.

Lurianic Kabbalism is virtually unknown to followers of the Western Tradition of Kabbalism. Western Kabbalists were most concerned with the Tree of Life and the sephiroth. This is part of, but by no means the totality of, Jewish Kabbalah. The Tarot also became intimately involved with Western Kabbalism and the Tree of Life. Jewish Kabbalists abhor the Tarot. They will not talk about it.

This, in a nutshell, is the state of the Kabbalah today. Two main groups—the Jewish and the Western Kabbalists— essentially do not know each other.

Jewish Kabbalism and Western Kabbalism are two very different traditions. Western Kabbalah is an outgrowth of the crossover of bits and pieces of the Jewish Kabbalah into the non-Jewish world where it was combined with other traditions to form a synthesis that is generally referred to as Western Kabbalah. This crossover probably began in the twelfth century as Jewish Kabbalah began to shed its mystique of absolute secrecy and became better known among European Jews who passed it on to Christian neighbors.

## Western Kabbalism

Western Kabbalism seems to have begun to take shape during the Renaissance, combining Rosicrucianism, astrology, Sufi mysticism brought back from the Crusades, magic, alchemy, Christian mysticism, hermetics and, of course, Jewish Kabbalah.

Initially, it was taken up by the priests and the aristocracy. The Kabbalah afforded a legitimate area of study and a cover for Christians who wished to explore the occult without being accused of witchcraft and heresy.

By the mid-1800's, another piece of Western Kabbalism fell into place, this being the Tarot. Prior to this, the Tarot had existed as a fortune-telling system. The Tarot consists of seventy-eight cards. Fifty-six of these cards are similar to a modern deck of playing cards with 4 court cards for each suit —King, Queen, Knight, and Prince (or Princess) instead of three court cards. In addition, there are twenty-two picture cards called the major arcana. The point of connection for the Kabbalists were the twenty-two letters of the Hebrew alphabet. The source of the twenty-two cards of the major arcana is unknown. No doubt there were secret occult schools that taught of the connections between the twenty-two cards and the twenty-two letters of the Hebrew alphabet for some period of time.

Its first appearance in writing was in France in the 1850's in the famous occultist Eliphas Levi's two-volume *Dogma and Theory of High Magic*. Here Tarot was portrayed as being the basis of a transcendental system of expanding consciousness known as magic, founded upon the principles of Kabbalah. Needless to say, it created quite a storm.

The Hebrew Kabbalists never accepted the Tarot as having anything to do whatsoever with Kabbalah. It probably is based on the prohibition in the Ten Commandments against any paintings and graven images as well as rigidity of thinking. Although the Hebrew Kabbalah is built upon a numerological system wherein words, phrases, and ideas of equal numerical value were seen as having an inner connection (every Hebrew letter also being a number), they do not recognize any connection between these twenty-two picture cards and the twenty-two Hebrew letters. This is probably the main stumbling block between Hebrew and Western Kabbalists. I will not go into the pros and cons of each position here. A Hebrew Kabbalist is right when he says that Tarot is not part of the Kabbalah, just as the Western Kabbalist is right when he says it is. The Kabbalah they are each talking about is a different system than the other's.

The Western Kabbalah gained fame and notoriety in late nineteenth and twentieth century England in occult groups such as the Golden Dawn. Most of modern Western Kabbalism is directly based on the work of these English explorers who added Egyptian trappings to round out the system. Aleister Crowley, a graduate of the Golden Dawn, was able to show the universal connection of the Kabbalah with all other mystical and religious systems. Despite his controversial reputation, no man is more responsible than Crowley in pointing out the universality of Western Kabbalism. And, herein lies its great appeal. Whereas Hebrew Kabbalism is all but inaccessible except to a small group of devout Jews, and Taoist Yoga is steeped in Chinese symbolism, Western Kabbalism is universal in its ability to encompass all systems. Perhaps Western Tradition is a better term for it than Western Kabbalah.

The Western Tradition is still young compared to its Taoist and Hebrew brethren. It needs time to grow.

The Hebrew Kabbalah, in turn, is just beginning to emerge from a long period of dormancy. Modern scholarship by authors like Gershon Scholem have again given it legitimacy. Brilliant writers such as Aryeh Kaplan have made the study and practice of Kabbalah among Orthodox and Hasidic Jews once again fashionable after more than a century of neglect. Universities in Israel now have Kabbalah departments. It is proselytized on the streets of New York City by the followers of Rabbi Philip Berg. Slowly, it is coming to life as Jews seek to explore their mystical heritage. Perhaps, it is a reaction to their disillusionment with the "rational" world after the Holocaust. Perhaps, it is the beginning of a whole new experience. Time will tell.

# The Structure of
# the Universe

Upon the ultimate source of all things, both the Taoists and the Kabbalists are in complete agreement.

## Wu Chi and Ein Soph

All existence came out of nothingness. The Taoists call this ultimate source *Wu Chi (No Chi)*. The Kabbalists called it *Ayin* (Nothing) or *Ein Soph* (No End, No Limit).

*Wu Chi* or *Ayin* is the ultimate mystery of the universe. It is beyond the laws of science although modern physicists seek it with great passion. It is beyond all things. It is beyond all words and thoughts. It is beyond mind and beyond reality. It can be spoken about, but it cannot be spoken of. If you try and grasp it, you will fail. If you try to contain it within your mind, you will become unbalanced. If you think that you know it, you would be mistaken. It is the unknown.

In the beginning, there was nothing. There was no time, there was no space. There was no up nor down, there was no east nor west. There was no good nor evil, there was no life nor death. There was no male nor female, there was no positive nor negative. There was no higher nor lower, there was no heaven and there was no earth.

It is beyond the Tao because Tao is a word that can be spoken. It is beyond *Wu Chi* and *Ayin* for these too are words that can be spoken. Yet, if we did not have these words then we could not speak of it at all. And, herein, lies its great mystery and paradox.

We need words to describe this concept of ultimate, limitless nothing. Yet, the concept itself is a limitation of something that is limitless. The Kabbalist often referred to this limitless nothing as the *Ein Soph*. But, the words again are limiting.

*Wu Chi* and *Ein Soph* can be experienced but cannot be described. The route is meditation. Experiencing this nothingness is a profound mystical experience. Both Taoists and Kabbalists sought to reach it. To the shaman, it was the source of all three worlds, existing simultaneously in each, beyond the highest height of the upper world or the deepest depth of the lower world.

The real difficulty in description and what I have tried to point out is that the experience is beyond the verbal powers of the mind. To achieve it, the student must first cut off the verbal chatter in the mind. The Taoist used beautiful poetic phrases to refer to this serene inner state, such as "the land of nothing at all is the true home."

Aryeh Kaplan, a modern Lurianic Kabbalist, calls it *Chokmah* (Wisdom) consciousness. In either case, it is still a long journey from achieving silence to attaining *Wu Chi* or *Ein Soph*.

Without a great amount of training in the arts and skills of meditation, attempting to journey into Nothingness or the Unknown can be quite dangerous. Many a seeker has become lost in its endless enormity.

However, between the two systems, the Taoist system is much safer in approach. In Taoist Yoga, a great deal of work is done to "root" the student to the earth. Much of the training is physical as well as mental so that when the student begins to experience the higher levels, he will be able to come back.

To a degree, Western Kabbalism is also concerned with the rooting concept. But, the rooting is mental. Western Kabbalists do not have their own physical exercises and often do various forms of Hatha Yoga. Many are probably unaware of the physical exercises of Taoist Yoga as alternatives. Taoists practice *Tai Chi* and a whole host of other exercises that are best labeled *Chi Kung*. Since this book is a comparison of the different systems, the best I can say here is neither Western nor Hebrew Kabbalists have an equivalent system of their own. The shaman used drumming and dancing to root himself to the world to insure he would return from his journey.

The Hebrew Kabbalists had a different tradition of rooting. The aspiring Kabbalist must be rooted in the Law, the Torah, before he could study the mysteries of Kabbalah. To the Kabbalist, the quest was very holy. *Ein Soph* is the ultimate God, the Holiest of Holies. The Hebrew rooting was based more on moral character and less on exercise. The results were mixed. Some reached the highest heights, some went mad, too many of the greatest seemed to die young. To the Hebrew Kabbalist, the path was outward; coming back seemed to be a secondary goal.

After experiencing God as the Ultimate Source of all things, why would the seeker want to come back anyway? In *Tales Of Power*, the fourth book in Carlos Castenada's story of the teachings of a Mexican Indian shaman named Don Juan, we see that this tradition of the unknown and its danger was well known in the shamanic tradition. Don Juan tells his student

Carlos that only a few seekers survive the encounter with the unknown. This is because the unknown, or *Nagual* is so enticing that it is almost impossible to return to the "real" world, the Tonal, where there is noise, pain, and order. In either case the decision to return is made by something within us that Don Juan referred to as our Will. There is no way of knowing in advance what the outcome will be; to remain in the unknown or return to Earth.

Returning to Earth carries great responsibility. The shaman will receive a task which he must dedicate his life to performing impeccably. He must gain patience and freedom from anxiety or carelessness or he'll be cut down mercilessly by the sharpshooters from the unknown.

A Jewish Kabbalist who was able to return from the *Ein Soph* was generally referred to as a saint. Humility seems to be one result inherent to the Kabbalist, Taoist, and Shaman who truly encounters the unknown and returns. His or her life is changed forever. "He is the same yet different" is a Taoist description of this change.

But, encounters of this sort are reserved for the very few and should not serve to scare off the student. Western Kabbalah has a long, well laid out series of initiations that lead safely to exploring the unseen universe. There are many safeguards built into the system, one of which is time to sufficiently mature and change, to be able to withstand the experience. Such a person is referred to as an Adept or Magus.

In Taoist and Kabbalistic theory, it is the *Wu Chi* and *Ein Soph* respectively that is the source of all things (all of creation).

Western Kabbalistic theory speaks of three levels or aspects of nothingness. First, there is *Ayin* (Nothing), next there is *Ein Soph* (Limitless), then there is a third aspect called *Ein Soph Aur* (Limitless Light). This is perceived as a higher light that existed prior to creation. There is no conflict here with Hebrew theory except that Western Kabbalists see these distinctions as dogmatic, whereas to the Jews these distinctions are much more tenuous.

## Tai Chi and Kether

The Taoists and Kabbalists are in basic agreement on the next step. From *Wu Chi* or *Ein Soph* came the primal unity, the place where all things exist in an undifferentiated state. A place where no opposites exist. The Taoists call this Tai Chi. The Kabbalists, Western and Hebrew, call it Kether.

Much of the Hebrew Kabbalistic theory concerns the events that led to the emanation of Kether. As this body of knowledge expanded from earliest times until the mid-1500's, it became more and more complex reaching a height of complexity in Lurianic Kabbalism. Western Kabbalism, which derived basically from pre-Lurianic sources, avoids most of the philosophic complexities of the Hebrew Kabbalism and is much more accessible in its approach.

## The Sephiroth

The Kabbalah, both Hebrew and Western, view all of creation as a series of ten emanations proceeding out of Nothingness. An emanation is a projection. It is not a one-shot deal but a continuing process. In other words, if the emanations ceased, all of creation would cease. The *Ein Soph* exists outside and beyond creation. All of creation came about as the result of the emanation of ten sephiroth from out of the unknown.

Sephiroth can be conceptualized as containers or vessels for the emanations out of the *Ein Soph*. In a certain sense, we are talking about ten dimensions. As we proceed from the first to the tenth, the energy contained becomes more "dense" until the world of matter is reached in the tenth sephiroth. However, the original source remains unchanged and changeless.

Picture a lit candle. Before this candle are to be hung ten handkerchiefs. If you were to look through the first handkerchief, the flame of the candle would be veiled but the light passing through the handkerchief would be evident. As the second, third, fourth, etc., handkerchief were placed before the candle, the light passing through the handkerchief becomes dimmer and dimmer until upon reaching the tenth handkerchief the residual glow might be dim or not visible at all. Yet, the candle itself continues to burn with the same intensity. It is only the veils before it that appear to dim its light. As you pass through the veils toward the source, the light becomes brighter and brighter.

So it is with the sephiroth and the theory of emanations. Perhaps the most intriguing aspect of the sephiroth and the emanations is its apparent correlation with modern scientific thinking. Modern physics seems to agree that all of creation began with nothing. Then, there was the Big Bang from which our entire universe was created. The latest thinking involves subjects that are just as arcane as Kabbalah and Taoist Yoga, such as quantum physics, string theories, black holes, etc. Modern physics seeks a Unified Theory, one theory to tie together everything in the universe. In *A Brief History of Time* (Bantam Books, 1988), Stephen Hawking, often called the most brilliant theoretical physicist since Einstein, speaks of one possible unified theory. The theory itself, based on string theory, is much too complicated and unnecessary to explain here. Hawking says that space-time is highly curved and ten dimensional. But because of its vast scale, the curvature and dimensions can't be seen.

Ten dimensions, ten sephiroth. Science and mysticism attempting to explain the same phenomena. The emanations from out of nothingness is the Kabbalistic version of the Big Bang.

Lurianic Kabbalism in its description of how this came to pass rivals modern physics in its complexity. Lurianic Kabbalism also relies on the theory of evolution to make creation work and give it purpose. When evolution is completed, the universe will again be unified. Assisting this unification is the job of the Lurianic Kabbalist.

## The Three Elemental Forces

The first sephirah was Kether. Here all exists in unity. There are no opposites. From Kether, the next sephiroth Chokmah (Wisdom) was emanated. Kabbalists refer to Chokmah as the Father. Chokmah emanated the third sephirah Binah (Understanding). This is referred to as the Mother. The three uppermost sephiroth Kether, Chokmah, and Binah are called the supernals. They are the most powerful forces in the created universe. The rest of creation emanates from them.

Taoist thinking is in perfect agreement with the Kabbalists. The classic Taoist work, the *Tao Te Ching* of Lao Tsu, states:

> The Tao produced the One;
> The One produced the Two;
> The Two produced the Three;
> The Three produced all the myriad beings

The One is the *Tai Chi* (Kether). The Two are the *Yang* and the *Yin*. These two, Father and Mother, positive and negative are the equivalent of Chokmah and Binah. The three are the Three Pure Ones, the three elemental forces.

These three elemental forces became the Heavenly, or Universal, Energy, the Human Plane Energy, also called Cosmic Plane Energy, and the Earth Energy. These are Taoist names for our old shamanic friends, the Upper World, the Middle World and the Lower World. The Heavenly Energy is the energy that exists in space, the Human Plane Energy is the energy that exists on the surface of the earth. Earth Energy exists beneath the surface of the planet. In Taoist Yoga, the student learns to tap into each of these forms of energy. In their primal state, these three forces existed prior to the creation of our planet or even the physical universe. The entire universe and all contained within it is a manifestation of the interaction of these Three Pure Ones. There is a balance here.

The Heavenly Energy (*yang*) is balanced with the Earth Energy (*yin*). The intermediary is the *Tai Chi* (Unity), the point of balance (see Figure 2).

The Kabbalists knew of these three elemental forces. They were called the Three Mothers. The earliest known Kabbalistic text, the *Sepher Yetzirah*, devotes an entire chapter to the mysteries of the Three Mothers. The Hebrew Kabbalists believed the actual creation of the universe was carried out by the letters of the Hebrew alphabet. These letters were symbols representing the actual sounds or commands coming from God out of nothingness. Each letter represents a different type of information. Each letter is holy. The Three Mother letters were the letters Alef (א), Mem (מ), and Shin (ש). From them came the three primal elements. the *Sepher Yetzirah*, Chap. 3, Sec. 2, states:

> Three Mothers: Alef, Mem, Shin
> A great, mystical secret...
> And from them emanated air, water and fire.
> They are divided as male and female.
> Know, think and contemplate that fire supports water.

# The Microcosm

The next step in creation in the Kabbalistic system was the emanation of sephiroth four through nine. These six sephiroth taken as a group are referred to by Kabbalists as the Lesser Countenance (Lower Face of God, Microprosopus, or Microcosm). They are below the three upper sephiroth. Kether is the Upper Countenance, the Macroprosopus or Macrocosm; Chokmah is the Heavenly Father and Binah is the Heavenly Mother. Between the upper three and lower six is a gulf or abyss within which is found Daath (Knowledge). Daath is not a sephirah or emanation. It separates the upper divine sephiroth which are thought of as essentially beyond human understanding from the Lower Face of God (Microprosopus) which is within human understanding. This may seem an odd thing to say after all that has been written here, but in truth who can truly understand the force that is the universe as a unified body or the Mother and Father of all creation? Microprosopus, these next six sephiroth, are forces that are in balance or equilibrium with each other. We have the fourth sephirah Chesed (Love or Mercy) in balance with the fifth sephirah Geburah (Judgment or Severity). They represent the two poles of divine love and divine retribution (see Figure 3). Balancing Chesed and Geburah is the sixth sephirah Tiphareth (Beauty or Harmony). Tiphareth is a most important sephirah. It is the place where all the "lower" divine forces are in perfect balance. In Kabbalah, to achieve Tiphareth consciousness is to achieve enlightenment. It is the realm of the holy sages. Western Kabbalists refer to it as Christ Consciousness.

The seventh sephirah Netzach (Victory) and the eighth Hod (Glory) are difficult to understand from the translations

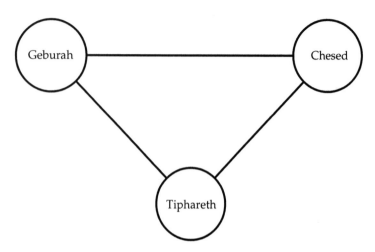

Figure 3: Tiphareth Balancing Chesed and Geburah

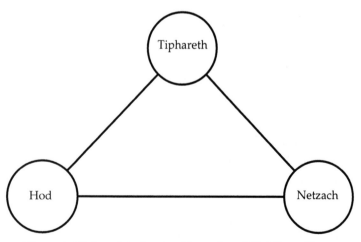

Figure 4: Tiphareth Balancing Netzach and Hod from Above

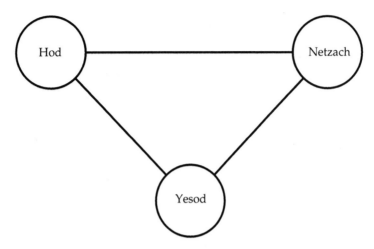

**Figure 5: Yesod Balancing Netzach and Hod from Below**

of their names. We are dealing with the underlying qualities of the universe. Netzach represents the force filling creation. It is thought of as the archetype for feeling and the emotions. Hod represents the concept of form or structure. It is the archetype of logic and rationality.

From above, *Netzach* and Hod are balance by Tiphareth (see Figure 4). Harmony balances the power of logic and emotion. Tiphareth is central to the Microprosopus (sephiroth 4 through 9), so much so that Western Kabbalists often refer to Tiphareth alone as Microprosopus (Microcosm). This was probably a result of meditational practices of the Western Kabbalists which will be discussed in a later chapter.

Below Tiphareth and balancing Netzach and Hod (see Figure 5) from underneath is Yesod (Foundation). Yesod represents the concept of something below the surface, i.e. the Foundation of all things. It is the archetype of the unconscious and subconscious thinking that goes on below the surface of awareness. It also represents the force of sexuality in the universe.

**Figure 6: Malkuth as the Physical Universe**

The tenth and final sephirah is Malkuth (Kingdom). It represents the physical universe, the world of things, the Earth (see Figure 6).

The Taoists have a somewhat analogous system. They have an Early Heaven (Macroprosopus or Macrocosm) and a Later Heaven (Microprosopus or Microcosm) much the same as the Kabbalists.

## The Elements

The Taoist sees Later Heaven as the place where the five universal energy forces were formed out of the interaction of the Three Pure Ones. These five elements are fire, water, wood, metal, and earth. Everything in the universe is composed of these five elements in either a pure state or interacting with one or more of the other elements. The term element is difficult to define. It refers to energy in the universe. This energy had two poles—*Yin* and *Yang*, and five phases or activities generally referred to as elements.

The Kabbalists saw the first three elements, Fire, Water and Air, as emanations from the Three Mothers. The Hebrew Kabbalists were most concerned with these three elements. The element of Air is actually the equivalent of two of the Taoist elements: Wood and Metal. Air is seen as having two poles rather than being separated into two distinct elements.

Franz Bardon, the German Hermeticist said in *Initiation Into Hermetics* that Air has two poles. It mediates between Fire and Water. The *Sepher Yetzirah* confirms, numerous times, that Air acts in a mediator or balancing role. Bardon further says that in its job as mediator, Air assumes the quality of dryness from Fire and humidity (moistness) from Water to establish the dual poles. The two poles of Air are moist and dry. By this same manner of reasoning, Bardon fails to say that the two poles also take on the qualities of warmth (not hot) and coolness (not cold). Warm and cool are the two balancing poles of hot and cold. The two poles of the Air element should be 1) moist and warm and 2) cool and dry to act as mediator between Fire and Water.

I searched for a long time for this information. Without it I could not complete the correspondences between the five Taoist and four Western elements. The Taoist element Wood has the quality of being warm and damp. Bardon's description of one pole of the air element as humid would appear to match. Metal has the quality of being cool and dry. The other pole of the Air element in Bardon's system has the quality of dryness. Close enough. Thus with the Western element Air combining the Taoist elements of Wood and Metal the two systems, Chinese and Western could be perfectly correlated.

On the Tree of Life (see Figure 7) the Chinese element of Wood corresponds to the sephirah Chesed. The positive emotion of Wood is kindness. Chesed means mercy. Wood grows out of the earth. Chesed is the first sephirah below the abyss and signifies solidity as a concept which ultimately becomes solid in the sephirah Malkuth(Earth).

The Taoist element of fire corresponds with Geburah. The fire of Geburah is a traditional correspondence. Water corresponds with the sephirah Netzach, which is the sephirah of the emotions. The emotions are ruled by the Water element in Western Kabbalah.

Metal corresponds with Hod. Hod is the sephirah of rationality and intellect. Cool and dry is a good description of this state. Metal is one pole of the Air element, and the basic symbol for Air in the Kabbalah is the sword which is made from metal. The Taoist element Earth directly corresponds with Malkuth, the Sephirah of the Earth.

That leaves us with just Tiphareth and Yesod. In the Kabbalah, Tiphareth is the Sun, and Yesod is the Moon. The Sun and the Moon were often used in ancient Taoist texts to refer to various alchemical operations in which they were combined. They fit into Tiphareth and Yesod perfectly.

The basic formula in Kabbalah is the Tetragrammaton or four-lettered name of God. It is composed of four Hebrew letterss: Yod, He, Vav, He. Each letter was assigned an element. Yod (י) is fire, He (ה)is water, Vav (ו) is air, and the second He (ה) is earth. The Three Mothers stood before creation. The Yod He Vav He is all of creation. The Tetragramaton is often translated as Jehovah or Yahweh. A Hebrew Kabbalist would never pronounce this name. Legend says its true pronunciation was given by God to Moses when Moses received the Ten Commandments. The name was passed on to the

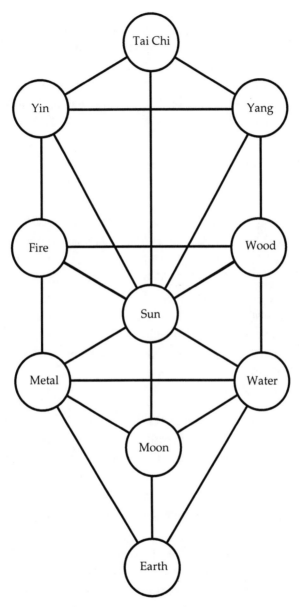

Figure 7: The Taoist Tree of Life

High Priest Aaron. This true pronunciation has been lost. Jews always substitute the name *Adonay* for Yod He Vav He when it is pronounced.

The universe of the Kabbalist is quite similar to the universe of the Taoists. The Kabbalist's universe was based on the number ten as manifest in the ten sephiroth. The *Sepher Yetzirah* says (Chapter 1, Sec.3):

> Ten Sephiroth out of Nothingness
> Ten and not nine
> Ten and not eleven.

The Taoist system is not quite so clear cut. However, if any number had to be chosen as the foundation of the system, it would be the number eight. *Tai Chi, Yin* and *Yang*, and the five elements add up to eight. The Tao and Confucian classic *I Ching* or *Book Of Changes* sees all that exists in heaven and earth as symbolized in eight trigrams. The universe is perceived as being in a constant state of dynamic change. The eight trigrams are the images of their movements in change.

## Chi and Akasha

One final aspect. The Taoist sees the universe as being filled with *Chi*, the unseen cosmic breath or life force. *Chi* takes many forms as does the Tao. Like the Tao, it cannot be fully defined.

The Western Kabbalists had a similar concept, the Akasha. It was seen as a fifth element that nourishes the other four. As such it was most similar to the concept of the *Ein Soph* as underlying all of reality.

This has been a brief view of the similarities of the structure of the universe as seen by the Taoists and Jewish and Western Kabbalists. It is by no means complete and is meant more as an outline.

## Shamanic Structure

The shaman generally had a mythological structure to his universe taking many forms and patterns. Their uniting features were the Upper, Lower and Middle Worlds and knowledge of the unknown source of all creation. Each culture had its own world view and mythology, but the basic structure was the same.

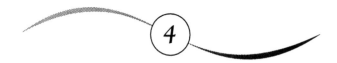

# Taoist Yoga

Taoist Yoga is not a religion. It is not synonymous with Taoism, which is a religion. It does draw on Taoist symbolism and was developed by Taoist sages, but essentially it is a coherent, methodical, esoteric system that requires no religious affiliation whatsoever. It also requires that the student not drop out of society, but in fact, remain an active and responsible member of his community able to support himself or herself as well as a family. There are no gurus, only teachers. Students are taught that they are their Own Master.

## Early History

For most of its history, its methods were secret. There were many different schools of internal alchemy. The early history consists of legends. The Yellow Emperor, Huang Ti (2698-2597 B.C.), was the supposed founder of Taoist Internal Alchemy. From thereon it was passed on orally until Ko Hung broke the taboo against putting the tradition into writing in his famous book *Nei Pien* in A.D. 320. Since that time, many hundreds of works were written by Taoist scholars. Almost none of these works were ever translated into English and those that were, like their Western alchemical counterparts, were highly inaccessible. This is always a problem when an oral tradition is put down in writing. Without the physical presence of a teacher to pass on the tradition, the words themselves often appear as little more than gibberish. The teacher gives life to and animates the process.

## Taoist Yoga in the West

In the West, Taoist Yoga was virtually unknown until the publication of *The Secret of the Golden Flower* in German in 1929 and in English in 1931. This was a mysterious text that spoke of the circulation of the light and the backward flowing method, the Elixir of Life, the Embryo of the Tao and the Immortal Spirit Body. The book contains a psychological interpretation by the world-famous psychiatrist, Carl Gustav Jung. It was translated and explained by the Chinese scholar Richard Wilhelm whose translation of the *I Ching* is still the classic work in the Western world.

Little else was written in English until Charles Luk (Lu Kuan Yu) included three chapters of Taoist self-cultivation in his book *The Secrets of Chinese Meditation*, published in England in 1964 and in the United States in 1969. Mr. Luk responded to reader's requests for more information on the Taoist school with his publication of *Taoist Yoga* in England in 1970 and in America in 1973. This book was actually a translation of a hundred-year-old Chinese text. By and large, this book contains a complete curriculum for Taoist Alchemy. However, in places it is incomplete and subjects appear out of context.

Learning Taoist Yoga from a book like this is a most dangerous and difficult undertaking as I myself discovered.

In China, Taoist Yoga was practiced either in secret societies or among the Taoist who generally lived in remote,
mountainous retreats, far from the workaday world. With the
Communist Revolution in China, many Taoists were forced to
flee from their ancient homeland and for the first time Taoist
teachers began appearing outside of China.

## *Mantak Chia and the Healing Tao*

Mantak Chia, born in Thailand of Chinese parents in 1944,
was an eighteen-year-old student when he began the study of
Taoist Yoga from just such a teacher. He continued his studies
until he became a master in his own right and established his
own school in Thailand in 1974. In 1977, he moved to New
York and opened the Taoist Esoteric Yoga Center, now known
as the Healing Tao Center. Mantak Chia is a prolific writer as
well as a tireless teacher. To date, he has published ten volumes on Taoist Yoga practices. What is most amazing about
Mantak Chia's teachings is his ability to strip away all the
flowery language and hidden meanings of earlier texts and
present a remarkably detailed, accessible, scientific approach
to this once arcane system. His books are committed to help-
ing the student understand. In addition, most of his teachings
are also available on audio and video tape. Mantak Chia was
the first person to openly teach Taoist Yoga in the West. In
1990, the International Congress of Chinese Medicine and *Qi
Gong (Chi Kung)* named him as the first recipient of the *Qi
Gong* Master of the Year Award. In China, these practices have
emerged again from obscurity to become a nationwide phenomena, making it all the more remarkable that a teacher in
America should receive its first-ever annual award.

The system of Taoist Yoga as taught by Mantak Chia is complex. I will attempt to outline it here.

It is important for me to note that, although Taoist Yoga or Taoist Internal Alchemy as Mantak Chia calls it, is a system that can be practiced by anyone, it is a Chinese system and its symbolism is Chinese. It never ceased to amaze me how alien in thinking some of the formulas were. Mantak Chia has so far done an outstanding job in presenting this mysterious Eastern system to the Western mind.

## The Chi Energy System

On a most basic level, Taoist Internal Alchemy is concerned with energy. First, a student learns to get in touch with and become aware of energy within his or her own body. This energy is called *Chi*. The student learns to direct the *Chi* energy through the two main energy channels in the body and form a circuit within the body. These channels are the acupuncture meridians. Chinese medicine, as practiced in China today, has an entirely different point of reference than Western medicine, yet it has been shown to be just as effective in most instances. The meridians or channels and the flow of energy through them is a given in Chinese medicine. This is, in large part, derived from shamanic and alchemical sources of both the inner and outer (actually changing lead to gold and gaining immortality by swallowing an alchemically produced Elixir of Life) schools.

## The Two Main Energy Channels

The two main energy channels are the Governor Channel which begins at the tip of the spine and runs up the back and neck, over the top of the head and down to a point behind the eyebrows finally reaching the top of the palate, and the Functional Channel which runs from the tip of the tongue, inside the mouth, down through the neck, chest, solar plexus, navel and past the genitals to the perineum, the point between the genitals and the anus.

Energy can flow in these channels in either direction. However, in most people these channels can be blocked or weak. The student is taught to bring *Chi* up from the base of the spine, up the Governor Channel, over the head and down the Functional Channel in the front of the body to the perineum (*Hui Yin*). This is called the Opening of the Microcosmic Orbit. The key to getting the orbit started is "thrown" by lifting the tongue to the roof of the mouth and thus completing the circuit.

## The Mind Directs the Chi

The flow of Chi is directed by the mind. The student generally begins to do the Microcosmic Orbit by concentrating on a point behind the navel. Much of the future work up to the intermediary alchemical formula known as the Lesser Enlightenment focuses on this point known as the *Tan Tien*. With a few weeks of practice, this navel center will begin to feel warm when the student concentrates on it. This warm feeling will move into the Microcosmic Orbit. This practice is often referred to as the Warm Current Meditation. At the end of a session which should last fifteen minutes or more (*The Secret of the Golden Flower* says a quarter-hour is sufficient), the concentration returns to the navel and energy is stored there in the *Tan Tien* by circulating the *Chi* around the navel.

## The Tan Tien

The *Tan Tien* is seen as the center of gravity of the body. Just as a fetus is attached to its mother by the umbilical cord at the navel, so too the practitioner of Taoist Yoga begins the process of attaching him or herself to the Earth and the infinite at the *Tan Tien* center behind the navel. Many spiritual practices talk about the need for centering; in Taoist Yoga this concept is taken literally.

The *Tan Tien* is at the center of the body. It's exact location differs in each person, but its general location is two to three inches directly behind and slightly below the navel.

The Taoists believed that when a human fetus was still in the womb, it received a special type of *Chi* through the umbilical cord. It was called Prenatal *Chi* and circulated freely in its Microcosmic Orbit as well as in all its thirty-two energy meridians. The fetus was maintained in a state of perfect health, growth, and equilibrium. After birth, the Prenatal *Chi* slowly loses its control over the body. As time passes, the *Chi* no longer freely circulates in the meridians and these meridians, or energy routes, become blocked, resulting in emotional imbalances, physical ailments, sickness and frailty in old age.

## Restoring Prenatal Chi

Two of the primary aims of Taoist Yoga is to restore the Prenatal *Chi* in the body, and get it to freely circulate in the energy meridians. The process is thus seen as one of rebirth, a return to that state of original perfect equilibrium. It begins with the opening of the Microcosmic Orbit (see Figure 8).

Thus, Taoist Yoga's first goal is to reestablish a healthy body and mind. Many students never seek the higher alchem-

The Functional Channel          The Governing Channel

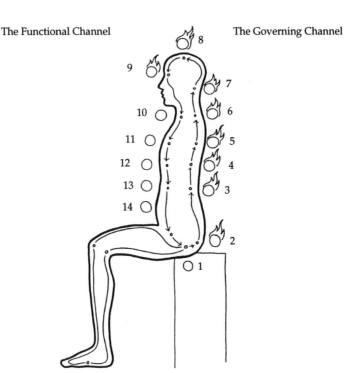

1. Hui-Yin (Perineum Gate of Death and Life)
2. Chang-Chiang, Coccyx (Sacrum Pump)
3. Ming-Men (Kidney Point; Door of Life): Pre-natal Energy Storage Safety Point
4. Chi-Chung (Adrenal Gland Center at T-11); Mini pump
5. Gia-Pe (Opposite of Heart)
6. Ta-Chui (Central Control of the Tendon Connections of the Hands and Spinal Cord)

7. Yui-Gen (Cranial Pump)
8. Pineal Gland at the Crown (Enlightenment Gland, Gland of Direction)
9. Pituitary Gland (Mid Eyebrow)
10. Hsuan Chi (Throat Energy Center)
11. Shan Chung (Thymus Gland) Rejuvenation Center
12. Chung Wan (Solar Plexus, Panres)
13. Tan-Tien (Navel Spleen)
14. Ovarian/Sperm Palace

**Figure 8: Opening of the Microcosmic Orbit**

ical practices at all. Along with the Microcosmic Orbit, the new student is taught to establish direct contact with his or her own internal organs. This contact with the interior of the body is of great importance in the Taoist system. Two initial methods are taught: the Inner Smile and the Six Healing Sounds. Both are also used as relaxation techniques and for stress reduction.

## *The Inner Smile*

The Inner Smile is a wonderful technique. The student learns to draw a happy smiling sensation into the eyes. The eyes are considered to be the two positive poles of the body, thus the

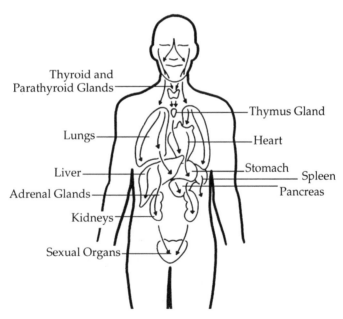

Figure 9: The Front Line Smile

work of transforming the body's negative energy into positive energy begins here. From the eyes, the smiling energy is directed down into the body in three "lines". The front "line" consists of the major organs: the heart, lungs, kidney, liver and spleen.

The middle "line" starts in the mouth and works its way down the throat and into all the organs of digestion.

The back "line" goes through the brain, then down the inside of the vertebrae of the spine, one by one. With a little practice it can be done rather quickly and the entire body begins to exude a positive, happy feeling. In addition, smiling through the eyes can work wonders on people you meet or

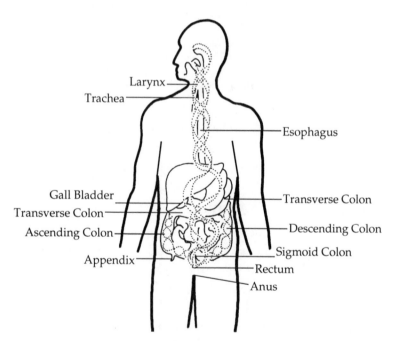

Figure 10: Smile down to the Digestive System

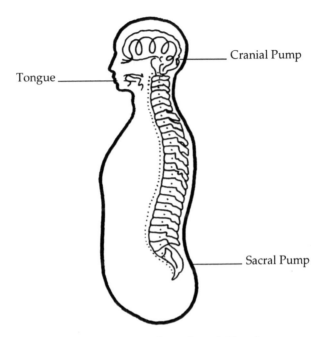

**Figure 11: Bring the Energy through Each Vertebrae**

deal with during the day. The Inner Smile is a powerful transformational technique. All the meditational practices that follow are enhanced if they are preceded by a quick Inner Smile.

## The Six Healing Sounds

The Six Healing Sounds are simple, vocalized sounds that are directed at the body's six major organs. The method is to breath in and concentrate on the organ. Slowly exhale and quietly make the healing sound, mentally directing the sound into its organ.

These sounds have a cooling and balancing effect on the organs and initiate the process of healing. They are: 1. lung sound—sssssss; 2. kidney sound—chuwaay (like the word chew sounded quickly, and way sounded slowly); 3. liver sound—shhhhh; 4. heart sound—hawwww; 5. spleen sound—whoooo; and, 6. triple warmer sound—heeeee (the triple warmer is not recognized as an organ in the west). It is performed by vocalizing, or vibrating the sound and feeling it move from the top of the head, like a wave, down to the sexual organs.

## Sexual Practice—Healing Love

Among the most secret of the Taoist practices was the use of sexual energy to augment the Microcosmic Orbit and other internal practices. Under the general heading of Healing Love, Mantak Chia calls this Seminal Kung Fu for men and Ovarian Kung Fu for women. In *The Secret Of The Golden Flower* it is called the backward-flowing method.

The sexual energy is called Jing. Normally, for men, this energy is lost during sex. However, the Taoist long ago discovered that the retention, turning back, and circulation of the Jing in the Microcosmic Orbit had an invigorating and rejuvenating effect on the body.

## Testicle and Ovarian Breathing

Two basic exercises are initially taught. First is Testicle or Ovarian Breathing. This gentle exercise teaches the student how to cause the Jing to rise from the genital region up the spine and into the higher energy centers, eventually arriving in the head to rejuvenate the brain. The second method is known as the Big Draw. This teaches how to keep from losing sexual energy during sexual intercourse. Obviously, the teaching is somewhat different for men and women.

The practice of Sexual Kung Fu is essential for the advanced alchemical disciplines. However, even in the beginning stages, their rewards are many, including greatly enhanced sex and total body orgasms.

Although both the Hebrew and Western Kabbalists had their own esoteric sexual practices, they arose in societies wherein sex was not a subject that was openly discussed. The Taoists had no such injunctions such as Original Sin and, as a result, the Taoist sexual secrets are perhaps the most sophisticated the world has ever produced, rivaling and often surpassing the better known Tantric Sexual Yoga that came out of India. These practices are more fully explained in a later chapter of this book.

## Iron Shirt Chi Kung

The student of Taoist Yoga will also practice physical exercises designed to help him move the *Chi* within his/her body. Iron Shirt *Chi Kung* teaches the student how to draw and circulate energy from the ground and store it in organs, tendons and fasciae (the connective tissue covering, supporting and connecting the organs and muscles). These exercises literally root the student to the Earth. This is absolutely vital to the higher practices. The higher the spirit climbs, the more firmly rooted to the Earth it must be.

The student is also offered other forms of exercise, such as *Tai Chi, Chi Kung*, Cosmic Healing *Chi Kung*, and Five Finger *Kung Fu*.

## Fusion of the Five Elements

It might come as a surprise that with all that has been described in this chapter so far, we have not yet reached those courses or formulas that would actually be considered alchemical. It is only when we arrive at those practices known as Fusion of the Five Elements that we begin the process of internal alchemy. It is taught in three steps: Fusion 1, Fusion 2, and Fusion 3.

The Taoists believe that the physical universe is composed of five different states of being or elements. These elements are not the same as those found in the periodic tables of first-year chemistry students. They are the five basic forms or phases that energy takes to make up everything that exists. The Kabbalists also have their own theory of the elements based on four, rather than five, elements. In China, this theory of the elements is still considered science. In the West, the scientific community long ago abandoned this theory as obsolete and pre-scientific. In truth, it is pre-scientific, but this does not detract from the fact that if they are understood in the context of what they mean within the Taoist or Kabbalistic system, they are quite coherent and logical.

The Taoists view the human body as a microcosm (or miniature) of the universe (macrocosm) in the sense that they are both constructed from the five elements. In the macrocosm, these elements are in a state of balance, and this is scientifically correct. Every atom, every electron, proton, neutron and every other subatomic particle exists in a state of balance in the known universe. This is a basic building block of modern physics. In the human body, the microcosm, we are born with the elements in balance, but as we grow toward adulthood, we lose this perfect balance. In order to return to the state of internal harmony, the balance must be restored. This is the purpose of The Fusion of the Five Elements formulas.

All five elements are in our bodies. They are contained in the major organs. When the energy from these organs is gathered and fused together, it has a harmonizing effect on the body. Our emotions are also controlled by the balance of the five elements within us, so that the Fusion practices will also harmonize our emotional state.

Each element governs a different emotion, both negatively and positively. One aim of the Fusion I practice is to convert negative emotions into positive emotions. The five elements of the Taoists are fire, water, wood, metal, and earth. They represent different energy states: fire is hot, water is cold, wood is warm and damp, metal is cool and dry, earth is neutral. These elements are assigned to five different internal organs. Fire is in the heart, water is in the kidneys, wood is in the liver, metal is in the lungs and earth is in the spleen.

This introduces us to the theory of correspondences; one thing or concept having a relationship or correspondence with another. Each element has many correspondences. For instance, fire corresponds with heat. In the body, it is found in the heart, its color is red, its season is summer, its negative emotions are impatience, hastiness and cruelty, its positive emotions are joy and respect. There are many, many more. Some are obvious, others are not. They have been worked out over millennia. Without them, the system doesn't work. The Kabbalah has its own system of correspondences. Often, they are different from the Taoist correspondences. But, the fact that both the Taoists and Kabbalists use correspondences as a cornerstone of their system is in itself a major correspondence between the systems.

## Inner and Outer Fusion

An important set of correspondences in the Fusion formulas is the inner organs to the outer external organs. The inner organs, the heart, kidneys, liver, lungs and spleen, are considered Yin,

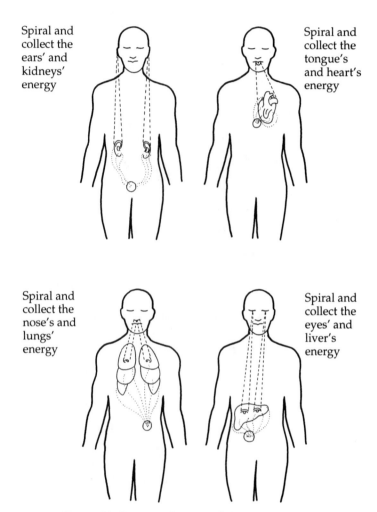

Spiral and collect the ears' and kidneys' energy

Spiral and collect the tongue's and heart's energy

Spiral and collect the nose's and lungs' energy

Spiral and collect the eyes' and liver's energy

Figure 12: Drawing the Five Elements to Tan Tien

Spiral and collect the mouth's and spleen's energy

Draw and combine the energies of all the senses and organs in the cauldron

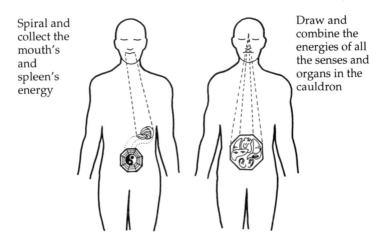

Figure 13: Final Steps in Drawing the Elements

or receptive, organs. They have their Yang, external counter-parts in the tongue, ears, eyes, nose and mouth, respectively. During guided meditations, the student will learn to connect the inner with the outer by putting their concentration first on the external organ, and then on the internal organ. It is some-thing that is indescribable to feel the ears listen down and connect with the two kidneys, or to feel the connection between the heart and the tongue. When you do the exercise, you feel it. A basic knowledge of anatomy is obviously impor-tant. You can't connect organs if you don't know where they are. Mantak Chia always has large anatomy charts and models of the human body with removable organs when he teaches to demonstrate their exact location.

In Fusion 1, the main collection center for the five ele-ments is in the *Tan Tien*, the point behind the navel. Energy from the heart, kidneys, liver, lungs and spleen, supplying all five elements, are collected and then mixed in the *Tan Tien*.

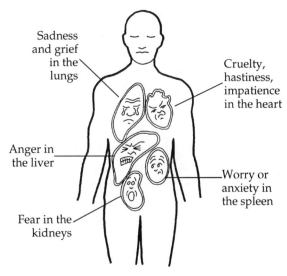

Sadness and grief in the lungs

Cruelty, hastiness, impatience in the heart

Anger in the liver

Worry or anxiety in the spleen

Fear in the kidneys

**Figure 14: Negative Emotions and the Organs**

Each element has its own collection point. Energy from the kidneys, Water, is collected in a three-inch circle at the perineum, the point between the genitals and the anus. Heart energy, Fire, is collected in a three-inch circle in the middle of the chest, between the nipples. Liver energy, Wood, is collected in a circle below the liver to the right of the navel. Lung energy, Metal, is collected on the left side also at the navel level. Spleen energy, Earth, is collected directly into the *Tan Tien* which is the Earth collection point.

The five elements are mentally drawn into the Tan Tien navel center. First, Water is collected at the perineum, then Fire is collected at the heart center. Both are simultaneously drawn into the Tan Tien, and mixed there. Next, the Wood energy is collected at the right side of the navel, then Metal energy is collected at the left side of the navel. Both of these are then simultaneously drawn into the Tan Tien and mixed with the Water and Fire.

Lastly, the Earth energy is collected directly into the Tan Tien. All the energies are mixed together in the navel center. Then, this blended energy is circulated in the Microcosmic Orbit.

There are many variations of this exercise. The outer organs are mentally connected to the inner organs before the energies are collected in the most basic variation. Each element corresponds to certain negative emotions. Water corresponds to stress and fear, Fire to impatience and cruelty, Wood to anger, Metal to sadness and depression and Earth to worry and anxiety. Just as set out above, the negative emotions are collected at their respective collection points then mixed in the *Tan Tien*.

It should be clearer now why the Fusion I exercises are also referred to as meditations for transforming negative emotions. The mixing and blending in the *Tan Tien* has a harmonizing and balancing effect on the organs and the emotions. At first, the effects are subtle, hardly noticeable. But, gradually you find that you are calmer, less anxious, more in command of your emotions. In a word, centered. Literally. You have created a laboratory at your body's center of gravity for the transformation of your body's own energies. The inner alchemical process has begun.

## Controlling Effect of the Elements

The five elements have a controlling effect upon each other. The weaknesses in the elemental balance can be discovered by use of what is called the Control Cycle of the elements. Water controls Fire, Fire controls Metal, Metal controls

Wood, Wood controls Earth and Earth controls Water. If there is too much of a particular element, it can be "cut back" by use of its controlling element. For instance, let's say you are experiencing too much anger. Anger is the negative emotion of the Wood element associated with the liver. The Wood is controlled by the Metal. So, Metal energy from the collection point to the left of the naval is mentally drawn to the Wood collection point to the right of the navel. The net effect is to cut down the Wood energy and control the anger. This whole process can become quite creative as the elements can be consciously manipulated to create the "internal weather" of your choice. But, this is an illustration of an advanced practice. Initially, we are learning to harmonize our "internal weather."

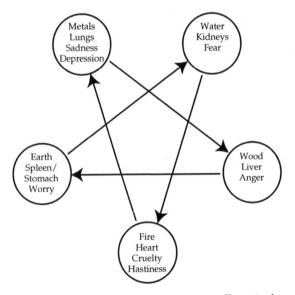

**Figure 15: The Counteracting or Controlling Cycle**

## Energy Body or Pearl

To assist in the collection process, a symbol known as a *Pa Qua* is formed at the *Tan Tien* navel center. The *Pa Qua* is an eight-sided figure originally based on the eight trigrams of the *I Ching*. It is a web-like pattern with the Tai Chi symbol at the center. Four Pa Quas are formed, front and back and left and right. All four symbols are then drawn into the Tan Tien, which in time will begin to glow and condense. This is the beginning of the formation of the energy body or pearl which Chia describes as "the highly condensed essence of your life force energy. It is the essence of your organs, glands, senses, and mind that will absorb the impure energy of the organs

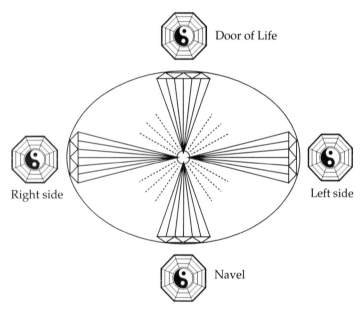

Figure 16: The Four *Pa Quas* and Condensing Energy into a Pearl

and glands, purify it, and return it to them as a higher form of energy." The pearl becomes a major tool in the meditations, and in the formation of a soul and, then, a spirit body outside of the physical body.

There are advanced Fusion 1 practices that I will not discuss now for fear of over-complicating this outline.

Mantak Chia has published ten books on Taoist Yoga as of the time that I write this. They are all excellent and well-thought out. However, he has not yet published books beyond the Fusion 1 level although he does outline, somewhat cryptically, all of the higher formulas in all his books. I will attempt to explain these higher formulas to the best of my ability. It should be remembered that up to now almost everything written about the alchemical formulas was anything but clear cut. Meanings were hidden, concepts were obscured and the language used was often that of metaphor. As you can see, the system is difficult enough when it is presented straight-forward. When it is obscured, it is impossible to comprehend.

## *Fusion of the Five Elements, Part 2*

Fusion 2 continues the work of the Fusion 1 practices. The student has learned how to collect the negative emotions and blend them into a more harmonious substance in the Tan Tien. This substance is the inner alchemical agent. Even at this point, we have just begun the true alchemical processes. Many steps lie ahead before the inner alchemical agent is mixed with the outer alchemical agent. Now, we are concerned with transforming the negative emotions into their positive counterparts. We have new correspondences now, the positive emotions of the organs. For the kidneys, it is gentleness, the liver is kindness, the heart is joy and respect, the spleen is openness and fairness, and the lungs are right-eousness and courage. I have given them in this order inten-tionally because this is the order that they are circulated in the Creation Cycle.

## The Creation Cycle

The Creation Cycle is used to grow or create positive energy in the body. The Pearl, which we learned to create in Fusion I, is circulated between the collection points of the five organs starting at the kidney collection point where the student expe-riences the cold, Water energy as gentleness. Next, we move

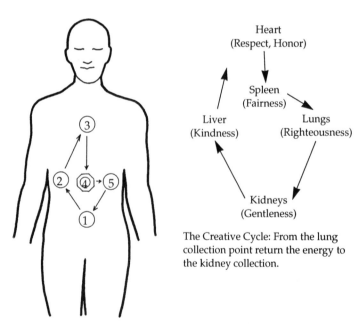

The Creative Cycle: From the lung collection point return the energy to the kidney collection.

**Figure 17: The Creative Cycle**

up to the liver collection point to the right of the navel and experience the warm and damp Wood energy as kindness. We move up to the heart and experience the hot, Fire energy as love, joy and respect in the collection point in the middle of the chest, which is also the location of the thymus gland. This gland plays a major role in Taoist alchemy. Its function is to start the regenerative process in the organs. Joy from the heart moves straight down to the Tan Tien at the navel where the neutral, Earth energy is experienced as openness and fairness. The last point is to the left of the navel where the cold, dry Metal energy is experienced as the emotions of bravery and righteousness. From here, the energy moves down to the kidney collection point at the perineum and cycle starts again.

The circulation of the Pearl in the Creation Cycle has numerous positive effects on the body as well as the psyche. We are creating positive energy and positive emotions. Part of the transformational process is ethical. We are becoming better people. We have balanced and harmonized our negative energy and emotions. Now, we are moving to the realm of the higher emotions and higher energy. Unless we grow up emotionally, future progress will be stunted.

Oft-times, new students will learn all the advanced alchemical formulas but fail to establish the necessary foundation of internal harmony through the practice of the exercises I have been describing. In the long run, this will lead to futility and failure. In this case, patience is certainly a virtue. And, in case you've forgotten, patience is a positive emotion of the heart.

In Fusion 2, we also learn two new energy paths within the body: the Thrusting Routes and the Belt Routes. This is a continuation of the work begun with the Microcosmic Orbit and these two routes will now become the most important energy channels in the body.

## *The Thrusting Routes*

The Thrusting Routes go straight up the middle of the body, from the perineum (between the genitals and anus) to the top of the skull. The energy that we have been refining and growing is condensed into a "Pearl" at the navel and mentally directed down to the perineum. The Pearl is made to rise in three lines - left, middle, and right - each an inch and one-half away from the other. At first, the Pearl is brought up to the level of the breastbone. Up on the left, down on the left.

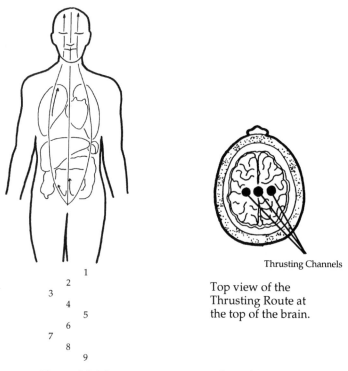

Thrusting Channels

Top view of the
Thrusting Route at
the top of the brain.

**Figure 18: Thrusting Routes Raised in Three Lines**
**(as numbered above)**

Then, up and down the middle and then, the right. Next, back to the middle, to the left, etc. The Pearl is raised and lowered nine times. Once this is mastered, the Pearl is then raised to the neck level and, eventually, the top of the head.

Throughout the teachings, Mantak Chia gives techniques to improve the practice. With the Thrusting Routes, as the Pearl is drawn up, you tighten the anus on the left, center or right, as appropriate, and the exercise becomes easier. Initially, the student might find these types of exercises take great effort to perform. The energy might be difficult to feel, or may seem unreal. Or you might not be able to get the energy to go where you want it to and it feels like it weighs a ton. Daily practice is required to overcome this. After awhile, the energy becomes easier to move, it feels lighter, and quickly goes where the mind directs it. The student will also continue to use the Sexual Kung Fu techniques to bring the Jing or Essence up to the brain. This strengthens the brain and makes it easier to control the Chi or energy in the other practices. After a while, it becomes fun to play with the energy ball, moving it through the many routes in the body.

## *The Belt Routes*

The Belt Routes circle the body like a belt, the primary Route being around the navel. The *Chi* is always circulated clockwise and counter-clockwise but, generally, not simultaneously in both directions. Usually six or nine revolutions in each direction will do. In all, there are ten Belt Routes: top of the head, mid-eyebrow, throat, heart, solar plexus, navel, midway between navel and genitals, coccyx, knees and feet. A practice session will usually begin at the navel and circulate six times counter-clockwise (from navel to left side, to back,

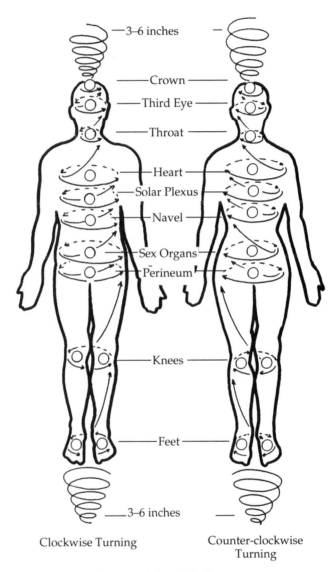

Clockwise Turning          Counter-clockwise Turning

**Figure 19: The Belt Routes**

to right side, and then back to the navel). Then, it is moved up to the solar plexus and again circulated six times counter-clockwise. The circulation continues in the same manner until the top of the head is reached. After completing the counter-clockwise circulation at the top of the head, the direction is then reversed to clockwise and circulated six times at all nine Belt Routes. When the feet are reached, you again switch to counter-clockwise circulation, and work your way back up to the navel where the exercise ends.

Initially, this exercise can be quite strenuous, but in time it becomes easy. Eventually, the student will dispense with the individual Belt Routes and simply "spin" an energy cocoon starting at the top of the head and working downward, clock-wise to the feet, then upward, counter-clockwise, to the top of the head. These routes are inside the body, and the *Chi* is circulated inside the body.

By this point in the training, we are becoming very profi-cient at moving energy through the body's energy meridians. We are circulating the *Chi* ball through the Governor and Functional Channels of the Microcosmic Orbit, up and down the center of the body in the Thrusting Channels and around the interior of the body in the Belt Channels.

## Fusion of the Five Elements, Part 3

In Fusion 3, we learn new energy meridians to add to our repertoire. Basically, we add in the arms and the legs in the Positive and Negative Arm and Leg Routes. The addition of these channels connects the entire body. They would sound very complicated if I tried to outline them in detail here. Basi-cally, it is as if we had split the Microcosmic Orbit into two separate lines of energy that can be moved independently or simultaneously. Most simply, we begin at the top of the skull, two points approximately two inches apart. The *Chi* is directed forward to the midpoint of the eyebrows on either side of the face. Then, down through the middle of the eyes and the cheeks to the two corners of the mouth. From there, down through the chin and neck to the base of the throat where they spread outward along the collar bone until they are above the nipples. From here, the energy travels down the front of the body in two lines until they reach the groin. The *Chi* travels down the inner thigh and calf, then circles around the inner ankles, up the inside of the foot to the big toes. From here, it moves to the middle of each foot, slightly backward to the base of the arch. This is the location of the "Bubbling Spring", the point where *Chi* can be drawn in or sent out of the feet. It is a most important spot and is essential for grounding the student to the Earth as well as in the Kan and Li formulas, when energy is drawn from the Earth. Next the energy goes forward to between the fourth and pinkie toe, then back along the outer foot circles the outer ankle and up the outer calf and thigh. When the two lines of energy reach the hip, they turn inward to points on either side of the spine about two inches apart. Now upward to the kidney point where the two lines begin to spread apart and move towards the shoulders and the outer arms. The *Chi* goes down to the outer elbow and outer wrist and then loops over the middle finger to the center of the palm, where it rests for a moment. Then to the inner wrist, inner elbow and inner upper arm up to the side of the neck to the back of the skull.

There is no question that when first learning the energy routes, they can seem like hard work and drudgery. But, once their locations are memorized and the *Chi* and *Jing* (sexual energy) is gathered and refined in the Fusion 1 and 2 and

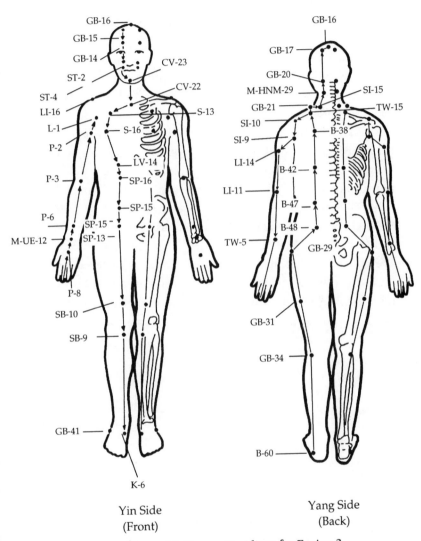

Figure 20: Energy Meridians for Fusion 3

Sexual *Kung Fu* exercises, energy can be moved through all these channels in just a matter of seconds. In fact, running energy through all the routes is an excellent way to get yourself going in the morning or any time you need more energy or to feel clearer.

Many other energy routes are taught in this course. We are beginning to have fun with the energy. We learn to project the Pearl above our heads to draw Heavenly Energy down, and below our feet to draw the Earth Energy up. We can surround our bodies with a *Chi* Aura for psychic self-defense and purification. We have become expert technicians in the gathering and refining of Jing (sexual energy) and *Chi* (life force energy). It is possible that the student has also learned how to breathe *Chi* directly into and out of the bones and flesh of the body in the Bone Marrow *Nei Kung* course. We are healthier, calmer, centered, and full of positive energy. Now, finally, the student is ready to deal with the real mysteries of internal alchemy which lead to the creation of the immortal spirit body in the *Kan* and *Li*; Lesser, Greater and Greatest Enlightenment.

～

# The Sepher Yetzirah
# and Franz Bardon

Mysteries within mysteries. This is the best explanation I can give of the true nature of the Hebrew Kabbalah. You can spend years studying the books and be a devout disciple of the Torah and you will still never get beyond the mysteries within mysteries.

These mysteries account for both the allure of and the fear of Kabbalah. There is no question that delving too deeply into the Kabbalah can be a shattering experience even for the initiated. Ah, but the rewards!

One of the most famous stories in Kabbalistic lore concerns the four great scholars; Ben Azai, Ben Zoma, Ben Yehuda and Rabbi Akiva. These Torah scholars lived in Jerusalem in the First Century A.D. after the destruction of the Second Temple by the Romans. Rabbi Akiva was the leader of this small group and he would guide them into mystical trances to explore the early Kabbalistic universe. According to historic accounts, after one such journey in which the group apparently delved deeper than ever before, Ben Azai's spirit entered the Light and never returned and his physical body died. Ben Yehuda saw two Gods, one good and one evil, returned and immediately renounced the Jewish faith. Ben Zoma went insane. Only the saintly Rabbi Akiva left and returned unchanged.

For most of its history, the Kabbalah was reserved for the few. A balanced mind and holy way of life were usually prerequisites to receive the secret, oral teachings. For the masses, it was generally considered too dangerous by both the Kabbalists and the orthodox religious leaders, who feared that rampant mysticism would lead the Jewish nation into idolatry and assimilation.

## Maaseh Merkabah: The Workings of the Chariot

The Kabbalah allegedly grew out of, and for a time coexisted with, another form of mysticism known as the Maaseh Merkabah, or Workings of the Chariot. These mysteries were derived from the prophet Ezekiel's vision of the Divine Throne:

> And above the firmament was the likeness of a throne, as the appearance of a sapphire stone and upon the likeness of the throne was the likeness as the appearance of a man above it. (Ezekiel 1, 26-28).

The Merkabah mystic would ride a chariot through the Seven Heavens and Seven Heavenly Mansions in his attempt to reach the divine throne of God. The route was immensely complex and fraught with danger. The chariot rider would be equipped with words of power and talisman and magical spells to gain entry to the heavenly abodes. He would prepare himself by fasting and chanting hymns and prayers. The traveler went on a shamanic journey first to the Lower and then the Upper World. The chariot was reached in a trance by means of a descent into the Lower World, and once reached, would be ridden to the Upper Worlds. These Seven Heavens and Mansions were inhabited by angels as well as demons who would wreak havoc upon the unprepared. In effect, the Merkabah mystic would unleash all the forces in his unconscious mind and, if he had not previously tamed his internal demons and paid proper homage to his angels, his trip through Heaven could quickly change to a nightmare in Hell.

The Merkabah mysteries were practiced from approximately 100 B.C. until 1000 A.D. They were considered so dangerous that, by the First Century A.D., the Jewish leadership decreed: "The discipline of the chariot may be taught only to individual students (one at a time), and they must be wise, understanding with their own knowledge."

Of course, there were those who did succeed in their quest and received the vision of the Throne of God. Often these visions were written down as guides for future travelers. The Throne vision was the aim of the Merkabah rider. He did not attempt to see beyond the Throne or question its nature or origin. This is basically what separated the Merkabah mystics from the early Kabbalists. The mysteries of creation and the true nature of the creator lay at the heart of the Kabbalah.

## The First Written Book of the Kabbalah

The earliest known written book of the Kabbalah is the *Sepher Yetzirah* which translates to *The Book of Creation* or *Book of Formation*. It is a very short book of six chapters that exists in a multitude of versions, all basically similar. As strange as this little book is, it is probably one of the most accessible of all true books of the Kabbalah. Most of the literature of the Kabbalah is philosophical in nature and requires a great deal of learning to comprehend. Rarely do we see any form of practice or system of meditation. This is not true of the *Sepher Yetzirah*. Here we find so much to practice and so many different meditational systems that it is difficult to decide where to begin. The book alters and changes according to one's perspective. Some of its interpretations are known, some are unknown, never having been put down in writing and the oral traditions are long lost. Some interpretations of the book bear a striking resemblance to Taoist internal alchemy, others bear no resemblance at all. One thing is for certain, the *Sepher Yetzirah* contains mysteries within mysteries.

## The Author of the Sephir Yetzirah

The true age of the book is unknown. In Chapter 6, it attributes its own authorship to the patriarch Abraham, the father of both the Jewish and Islamic nations. Although the ancient authorities accept this as true, many others claim it is only an example of pseudepigrapha (later authors attributing their work to earlier writers to give it more credibility and to maintain their own anonymity). However, there is good reason to believe that Abraham may well be the founder of the oral tradition that was eventually written down many centuries later as the *Sepher Yetzirah*.

Abraham lived approximately 3,800 years ago. He spent his life moving throughout the Middle East, Mesopotamia, Egypt, as well as what is now Israel. Rabbi Aryeh Kaplan, in his introduction to *Sefer Yetzirah*, says he was reputed to be the greatest mystic and astrologer of his age and was apparently an authority on the mystical and occult secrets of Egypt and

Mesopotamia. This is often overlooked by commentators on the *Sepher Yetzirah*. The original oral traditions are long lost. What does come down to us are later interpretations of this book. When examined as having derived in part from earlier Egyptian and Mesopotamian sources, the *Sepher Yetzirah* becomes even more mysterious because it is obvious that it contains an alchemical tradition that is apparently unknown to the Hebrew commentators, as well as an entire curriculum of practical Kabbalah (hermetics and magic) that Hebrew scholars don't ever discuss. Modern scholars such as Rabbi Aryeh Kaplan, whose excellent book of commentary entitled *Sefer Yetzirah* was recently posthumously published (Samuel Weiser, Inc., 1990), have done much to uncover the meditational aspects of the book, which in itself is a great stride forward, but aside from some reputed formulas for making a *Golem* (artificial man), the practical or magical aspects of the book are shunned. This is typical of all the modern Hebrew scholarship on the Kabbalah and is one probable reason that this type of work became the province of the Western Kabbalists. For the Jews, the Kabbalah became too rational and philosophical to include such subjects.

As written versions have come down to us, the *Sepher Yetzirah* includes concepts of the Throne of God that are part of the Merkabah Mysteries. But, if the book is really derived from ancient sources as I above derive, these were added at a later period rather than the Kabbalistic aspects being later amended onto the Merkabah mysteries. Many scholars believe that it was Rabbi Akiva, introduced at the beginning of this chapter, who was the first to set the *Sepher Yetzirah* down in writing in the First Century A.D. His methodology included Merkabah as well as Kabbalistic concepts, so his reputed authorship of the written version is not farfetched. It is reasonable to assume that he took the earlier oral tradition and added the then current and exciting methods of the Merkabah. Other scholars give much later dates for the actual writing down of the book. The truth is lost to history.

As a result of the *Sepher Yetzirah* originally being an oral tradition, different versions came into existence over the centuries. Most versions have six chapters and a basically identical structure. It is in the correspondences of the Hebrew letters that they differ radically. As to the meaning of the book, despite a wealth of scholarly commentaries, Gershom Sholem, the greatest modern scholar of Kabbalistic history, the man who salvaged the Kabbalah from the ash heap of forgotten history, is probably correct when he states, that most of the details still await a full clarification (*Major Trends in Jewish Mysticism*, page 77.)

## The 32 Mystical Paths

The *Sepher Yetzirah* describes the creation and maintenance of the universe by means of the numbers one through ten and the twenty-two letters of the Hebrew alphabet. They are introduced together as the thirty-two mystical paths of wisdom in the first line of the book. The ten sephiroth are then introduced and the twenty-two letters are further divided into three Mother, seven Double, and twelve Simple letters. The rest of Chapter 1 deals with the sephiroth that here make their first written appearance in history. Chapter 2 deals with the twenty-two letters. Chapter 3 describes the three Mother letters.

Chapter 4 describes the seven Double letters and Chapter 5 the twelve Simple letters. Chapter 6 is something of a summary with some new material and the attribution of Abraham in the last paragraph as the author.

I don't intend to go through the *Sepher Yetzirah* line by line. Nor do I intend to review the research of others. Most of the known practices of the Jewish Kabbalists are so seeped in Judaism and the permutations and unifications of the letters as to be beyond the understanding of the more general reader. I don't mean this in any derogatory sense. It is simply too esoteric for all but the Hebrew Kabbalist. I refer the interested reader to Aryeh Kaplan's superb *Meditation and Kabbalah* (Samuel Weiser, Inc., 1982) and *Sefer Yetzirah* (supra). Rabbi Kaplan, in his short life (48 years), did more to revive the almost lost art of Hebrew and Kabbalistic meditation among late twentieth century Jews than any other man in the past 150 years. I commend his spirit to Heaven.

## *The Alchemical Tradition*

I do intend to explore some hitherto unknown and obscure avenues, beginning with alchemy. There is no reason why the rabbinical commentators would have had any knowledge of this rather specialized practice. Somewhere in antiquity, the line of the teacher, or teachers, who knew the alchemical tradition died out without ever being committed to writing. This could even have occurred before the time of Moses. I really don't know. Gershom Sholem, in his monumental treatise *Kabbalah* (Keter Publishing House, 1974) states that the Zohar alludes to a harmonious relationship between Kabbalah and alchemy. He also reports that at the time of the expulsion of the Jews from Spain (1492), Joseph Taitazak declared alchemy to be identical with the divine wisdom of the Kabbalah. What I can say with certainty is that there are references in the *Sepher Yetzirah* that are generally referred to as obscure and whose obscurity disappears once their alchemical meanings are

understood. I don't mean to imply that this is the "true" interpretation or the only "authentic" meaning. The *Sepher Yetzirah*
contains levels within levels, meanings within meanings and
mysteries within mysteries.

## Taoist Internal Alchemy

As we learned in the chapters on Taoist internal alchemy, the
process of internal alchemy actually begins with the Fusion
exercises. This is when we learn to work with the elements.
This type of elemental work was well known in Western
antiquity where it was referred to as the science of Hermetics,
derived from the name of the legendary Hermes Trismegistus,
supposedly the greatest of all the Egyptian scientists and
occultists as well as being the wisest man of his age.

A complete mastery of Hermetics was necessary before
the mysteries of internal alchemy were attempted. This in
itself was a long and arduous task. However, once the science
of the elements was mastered, the student could then move
on to the deeper mysteries of the Kabbalah as well as Inner
Alchemy. These deeper mysteries involved mastery of the letters and numbers of the thirty-two paths. I will attempt to
describe this rather complex system to the best of my ability.
It is a reconstruction of the Kabbalah that is essentially different from the philosophical, analytical Kabbalah of *The Zohar*
and Isaac Luria or the *Sepher Yetzirah* derived letter permutations of Thirteenth Century Abraham Abulafia.

We begin with the Three Mother Letters: Aleph (our letter A), Mem (M) and Shin (Sh). It is upon these three letters
that the entire hermetic and alchemical system of the *Sepher
Yetzirah* is based. As previously mentioned in the chapter on
the Structure of the Universe, the Three Mother Letters each

emanated and correspond with an element. Aleph is air, Mem is water and Shin is fire.

The primary aim of all hermetic systems, including Taoist alchemy, is to balance the elements. The three Mother Letters are twice compared to a scale or balance, "on the one hand a pan of merit and on the other a pan of sin and the Aleph is like the tongue of the balance standing between them" (Chap. 2 Sec. 1 and Chap. 3 Sec. 1).

The letter Aleph emanated the element Air. Air is repeatedly portrayed as the mediator between the two other elements, Fire and Water, in a series of correspondences in Chapters 2, 3, and 6. Twice it is described as the tongue of a set of scales. The image here is the traditional Scales of Justice. When the two opposing forces of merit and sin or good and evil are in balance, the Tongue of the scales points upward in a state of equilibrium. It is this point of equilibrium which is crucial. Without the establishment of equilibrium no real progress can be made. Without balancing and harmonizing the elements, we are in a state of chaos, different elements predominating at different times.

The *Sepher Yetzirah* provides an entire course in balancing the elements by use of the Three Mother Letters. In essence, the teachings are quite similar to Taoist Internal Alchemy. It is important to learn the basic correspondences of the letters for the system to make sense.

We are told that the Three Mothers operate in the Universe, in the Year and in the Soul, male and female. Basically, it is saying that the Three Mothers are at work in space, time, and within humankind.

In the Universe (space), Heaven was created from Fire, Earth was created from Water and Air was created from the Breath of God.

In the Year (time), there is the hot, cold, and temperate times. The hot is created from Fire, the cold from Water, and the temperate from Air.

In the Soul, male and female (humankind), the head is created from Fire, the belly (abdomen) from Water, and the chest from Air.

In Chapter 2, Sec. 1 and again at 6:2, it is stated "Fire is above, Water is below and Air of Breath is the rule that decides between them." Then, that most mysterious line, "And a sign of this thing in that fire supports water," which appears to contradict the previous line that fire is above and water below.

## Kan and Li Alchemical Formulas

How do we explain this sudden inversion of the elements? Chapter 3, Sec. 2 (Long Version) states: "Know, think and contemplate that fire supports water." Advanced students of Taoist Alchemy recognize this to be the basic formula for all the *Kan* and *Li* alchemical exercises. *Kan* is Chinese for Water and *Li* is Chinese for Fire. Normally, in both the Taoist and Kabbalistic systems, Fire is in the upper part of the body and water is in the lower part of the body. For the Kabbalists, it is Fire in the head, the letter Shin, and Water in the abdomen, the letter Mem. For Taoists, it is Fire in the heart and Water in the genital region.

The *Kan* and *Li* formula reverses the position of these two elements. The Fire element is brought down from the heart and the Water element is brought upwards from the genitals until the Water is above the Fire. The two elements are then brought together. A cauldron is pictured. The Water goes into the cauldron and the Fire is placed below the cauldron

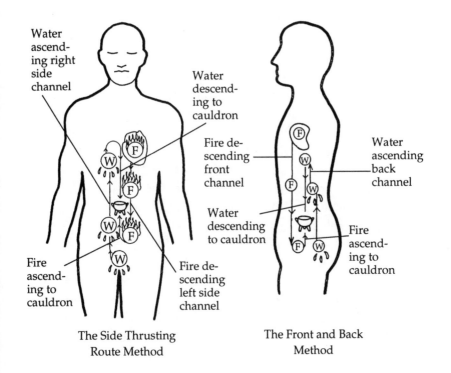

Water ascending right side channel

Water descending to cauldron

Fire descending front channel

Water descending to cauldron

Fire ascending to cauldron

Fire descending left side channel

Water ascending back channel

Fire ascending to cauldron

The Side Thrusting Route Method

The Front and Back Method

Figure 21 : *Kan* and *Li* Formulas

heating it up. Eventually, the Water begins to boil and steam is given off. This steam is one form of what is referred to as an inner alchemical agent.

To return to the *Sepher Yetzirah*, it is now obvious what the phrase "and fire supports water" means. It is the basic universal formula for internal alchemy. It doesn't belong anymore to the Chinese than it does to the Jews. It is the Basic Formula of Alchemy. I just wanted to point out that it is in the *Sepher Yetzirah*. I've never seen any mention in any book of commentary that this was so. But, it is there and, somewhere in antiquity, this was taught, but the line of teachers disappeared. One most favorable condition of living in these modern times is the free exchange of information. Until 1983, when Mantak Chia first taught Lesser Enlightenment *Kan* and *Li* at a summer retreat in Kerhonkson, New York, this information was unknown in the West. And now, as so often happens, an ancient oriental secret tradition is found to have an exact counterpart in the West. Fire supports Water. Since Abraham, the alleged author of the *Sepher Yetzirah*, was knowledgeable of the mysteries of the Middle East and Egypt, (a literal translation of alchemy is roughly "the Egyptian matter") it would seem likely that the alchemical formula was being practiced before the time of Abraham. Taoist Alchemy is reputed to be over 6,000 years old, at least 2,200 years before the birth of Abraham. Perhaps there is a common source here, carried over ancient trade routes between the Middle East and China. No one will ever really know.

## Lost Traditions of the Sephir Yetzirah

So what are we to make of all this? Aside from the alchemy, the analogy to the Upper, Lower, and Middle Worlds of the shaman should be obvious: Fire in the Upper World, Water in the Lower World, and Air in the Middle World. We can see that at least part of the *Sepher Yetzirah* appears to derive from some ancient shamanic based tradition. Remember that the 90,000 year old *homo sapiens* bones mentioned in the first chapter of this book were found in Israel. There is good reason to believe that the shamanic tradition goes back at least to the time of the birth of modern man. It is likely that a more advanced concept of life, the universe and the spiritual world was one of the major differences between the later *homo sapiens* and the earlier Neanderthal man.

## Franz Bardon

But still, so what if there is an alchemical and shamanic foundation to the *Sepher Yetzirah?* The answer is that these aspects have been lost by later interpreters. The book contains an entire outline of a very elaborate alchemical-shamanic based system. Few writers or scholars seem to be aware of this. One person who was learned in just such a tradition was Franz Bardon, a German Kabbalist and hermeticist who died in 1958. A most remarkable man, he revealed in his three completed books a magical universe unlike anything previously published in their openness and desire to provide the means and explanations to explore the mysteries. His book *The Key to the True Quabbalah* (Dieter Ruggeberg, 1957) is an absolutely stunning and totally unique approach to the subject matter. For years, I could not fathom the source of his information. Then, with the publication of Aryeh Kaplan's *Sefer Yetzirah* in 1990, I was finally able to put some pieces of the puzzle together. In *Sefer Yetzirah,* Aryeh Kaplan actually translates four different versions of existing texts into English. One version known as the Short Version (because it's shorter than the others) contains correspondences for the remaining nineteen letters of the Hebrew alphabet (other than the Three Mother Letters) that differ in the whole from the other versions. I had made a chart of all the correspondences in Bardon's Quabbalah and found that almost all matched the correspondences in the short version of the *Sepher Yetzirah*. Considering how different the correspondences in the various versions could be, I found that Bardon and the Short Version presented remarkable consistency. For instance, in the Gra version of the *Sepher Yetzirah*, the Double Letter "Peh" corresponds in mankind with the left ear, while in the Long Version "Peh" corresponds with the left nostril. In the Short Version, it's the right nostril. In Bardon, the letter "P" (the equivalent of "Peh") corresponds with the right nostril. This happens in eighteen out of the possible twenty-two Hebrew letters. Of the other four, two are inverted and two are different. The overall connection between the two books, Bardon's *Key to the True Quabbalah* and the short version of the *Sepher Yetzirah* is not to be denied. Yet, there are certain differences. Bardon's system had added certain correspondences that are not mentioned in the *Sepher Yetzirah* such as color. But, there is no question that much of his Quabbalah as well as his first book *Initiation Into Hermetics* (Dieter Ruggeberg, 1956) are derived from a course of study based on the *Sepher Yetzirah*. Bardon claims that the system is thousands of years old and that it does derive from the "Sepher Jetzirah".

In order to make progress with the *Key to the True Quabbalah*, the student must first have mastered most of the lessons in Bardon's first book *Initiation into Hermetics*, which deals in large part with mastering the elements.

## Comparison of Bardon and Sepher Yetzirah (short version)

| CORRESPONDENCES | | | BARDON | SEPHIR YETZIRAH |
|---|---|---|---|---|
| ENGLISH | HEBREW | MATCH | | |
| A | א | Yes | Lungs (Chest) | Chest |
| B | ב | Yes | Right Eye | Right Eye |
| G | ג | Yes | Left Eye | Left Eye |
| D | ד | Yes | Right Ear | Right Ear |
| H | ה | Yes | Right Arm (Hand) | Right Hand |
| F | ו | Yes | Left Hand (Arm) | Left Hand |
| Z | ז | No | | Right Leg |
| CH | ח | Yes | Left Leg | Left Foot (Leg) |
| T | ט | Yes | Right Kidney | Right Kidney |
| I | י | Yes | Left Kidney | Left Kidney |
| K | כ | Yes | Left Ear | Left Ear |
| L | ל | No | Spleen | Liver |
| M | מ | Yes | Abdomen | Abdomen |
| N | נ | No | Liver | Spleen |
| S | ס | Yes | Gall | Gall |
| O | ע | Yes | Throat | Throat |
| P | פ | Yes | Right Nostril | Right Nostril |
| R | ר | Yes | Left Nostril | Left Nostril |
| U | צ | Yes | Solar Plexus | Solar Plexus |
| C | ק | Yes | Stomach | Stomach |
| SH | ש | Yes | Brain | Head |
| TAV | ת | No | | Mouth |

Figure 22: Comparing systems from Franz Bardon
and the *Sepher Yetzirah*

I propose that this system is closer in nature to the original intent of the *Sepher Yetzirah,* as it was orally transmitted long before it was ever written down. Later writers tended to interpret the *Sepher Yetzirah* in terms of the current popular philosophic and Kabbalistic outlook and little by little its original meaning became lost. This is particularly true in Aryeh Kaplan's commentaries in his *Sefer Yetzirah.* He gives us eighteenth-century Hassidic interpretations as well as those of sixteenth-century Issac Luria and the classic Kabbalists of the twelfth, thirteenth, and fourteenth centuries, etc., but completely missing is the original oral tradition. The reason for this is that it was lost. The very fact that Bardon's work is so different from other interpretations, yet is so similar in many ways to Taoist Internal Alchemy, which is a very ancient system itself, leads me to believe that we may well have a remnant of the original tradition here. In any case, it provides food for thought and a practical and methodical approach to the teachings of the *Sepher Yetzirah.* This system is basically universal in approach and doesn't require an encyclopedic knowledge of Hebrew mysticism to understand.

## Further Mysteries of the Three Mother Letters

Based on a knowledge of Bardon's system and Taoist Internal Alchemy, when we return to our discussion of the Three Mother Letters, some of the mystery drops away.

In Chapter 1:1 of the *Sepher Yetzirah* there is a further reference to the number Three. We are told that the universe was created with letters, numbers, and sounds (speech). These are called collectively the Three Sepharim, or Three Books. Aryeh Kaplan states that the letters, numbers and sounds (he translates them as text, number, and communication) correspond to the three divisions of the Mother Letters; Universe, Year, and Soul, respectively, and represent the aspects of quantity, quality, and communication.

## The Power of Sound

We are being told that aside from the letters and numbers from which the *Sepher Yetzirah* was composed, sound is also a key to the mysteries.

Then, in Chapter 2:1, we are told Mem hums, Shin hisses and Aleph is the breath of air mediating between them. This is the beginning of the training with the Three Elements. We learn the sound of the Three Mothers. Mem is hummed: m-m-m-m-m; Shin is hissed: sh-h-h-h-h; and Aleph is sounded like a breath of air: ah-h-h-h-h.

We now learn to associate each sound with its element: Sh-h-h-h-h with fire and heat, m-m-m-m-m with water and cold, and ah-h-h-h-h with air and a neutral, temperate temperature. These exercises must be developed over a period of time. The student must actively imagine that when he makes the sound sh-h-h-h-h, for instance, that he actually feels heat. After time and continued practice, he will feel heat; likewise, for the two other elements, until the sound is fully linked to the proper temperature.

The next step is to associate each sound with the proper corresponding part of the body: sh-h-h-h-h with the head, ah-h-h-h with the chest, and m-m-m-m-m with the abdomen. When we make these sounds, we can feel their effect in these various parts of the body. This process is quite similar to the Taoist exercise Six Healing Sounds. With the Six Healing Sounds, various organs are calmed, relaxed, and cooled down by use of the various sounds. With the Three Mother Sounds, we are dealing with the more generally defined body parts of head, chest, and abdomen. We could call them the "Three Healing Sounds."

The work must continue until the student can feel heat in the head, a neutral temperature in the chest, and cold in the abdomen when sounding out the letters.

The sounding out of the Three Mother Letters also serves as a form of mantra. The letters are slowly pronounced and the student allows his consciousness to descend from the head down into the abdomen (as in the Taoist Triple Warmer). This mantra, sh-h-h-a-a-h-h-m-m-m, also promotes internal silence. As the consciousness moves down to the abdomen, the internal dialogue that so many students experience as an interference to meditation, is cut off. At first, this effect is momentary. With the point of consciousness removed from the head and lowered into the abdomen, there is a cessation of the constant chatter in the brain. However, this effect can be quite startling to the student and his conscious mind will generally take over with thoughts like "it's so quiet in here." Practice is required. The student is so used to the habitual presence of the "chatterbox" in the mind that when it turns off, the experience can be quite frightening. It feels as if a part of you is dying. This internal dialogue is often mistaken for the self. It is not. It is merely interference and the sooner it is brought under control, the sooner the student can make further progress.

## Balancing the Elements

In effect, all these exercises mirror Taoist Internal Alchemy. By lowering the consciousness into the abdomen, we enter the realm of the lower *Tan Tien*, where the exercise of the Microcosmic Orbit begins and where the elements are gathered in the Fusion exercises as well as where the elements are inverted for the Lesser Enlightenment.

The element exercises of the *Sepher Yetzirah* are designed to balance the elements in the body. I've just set out a few of them here. Franz Bardon devotes a major part of his *Initiation Into Hermetics* to various element exercises. This westernized system differed in structure from the *Sepher Yetzirah* in that Earth is seen as a separate element, whereas in the *Sepher Yetzirah*, Earth is seen as being created from Water and is not seen as a separate element. This can be explained in that in Kabbalistic theory, the universe was seen as having been created in four stages. These are referred to as the Four Worlds of Atziluth, Briah, Yetzirah and Assiah. Assiah is the physical universe (akin to Malkuth). Yetzirah is the world of formation (akin to Yesod) that underlies what is generally referred to as the real world or Assiah. In the world of Yetzirah there is no solidity and thus no element Earth. It is only in Assiah that solidity takes place and Earth exists as a separate element.

In the *Sepher Yetzirah* every one of the twenty-two Hebrew letters corresponds with a body part or organ. The three mother letters *Shin, Aleph*, and *Mem* refer to the head, chest, and abdomen, respectively. In addition to the Three Mother Letters, there are also the Seven Double and Twelve Simple Letters. Each of these letters also referred to various body parts. Unfortunately, the *Sepher Yetzirah* is devoid of instructions of what to do with the information. It often seems that it resembles a student's outline notes culled down to the bare essentials rather than a transcription of the full original teachings. The need for secrecy in ancient times was probably the underlying reason for this. A simple first reading of the *Sepher*

*Yetzirah* will generally leave you scratching your head. However, when it is examined with an open mind, without relying solely on traditional Hebraic interpretations, it becomes obvious that here is an entire esoteric mind and body as well as spiritual system.

## The Seven Double Letters

The Seven Double Letters each had four different correspondences: 1) A body part, 2) a planet, 3) a day of the week, and 4) an attribute such as wealth, peace, wisdom, etc. According to Aryeh Kaplan, the attribute desired (such as wealth or wisdom) could be enhanced by use of the four correspondences. For instance, the letter *Gimel* (G) corresponds with 1) the left eye, 2) the planet Jupiter, 3) the day Monday, and 4) the attribute of peace. Kaplan says that to use this information one would meditate on the right ear, preferably on a Monday, and more preferably on an hour of the day when Jupiter predominates (a chart for doing this, derived from biblical sources is supplied by Kaplan in his book) so that one could achieve peace. In a real sense he is equating these teachings with magick, which was defined by Aleister Crowley as "the science and art of causing change to occur in conformity with will" (*Magick in Theory and Practice*, Castle Books, pg. XII, undated). Anyone with a knowledge of medieval magical grimoires (books of magical formulas and instructions), such as *The Key of Solomon* and *The Lemeggeton*, would immediately recognize the methodology, i.e. casting a spell on the proper day at the proper hour for the proper purpose.

## The Twelve Simple Letters

One might be surprised to find apparent astrological associations here in one of the most sacred books of the Kabbalah. But that is just what they are. If we continue with the final twelve letters of the Hebrew alphabet, the Twelve Simple Letters, we find that each one corresponds to a sign of the zodiac (*Heh* (H) is Aries, *Vav* (V) is Taurus, etc.). Astrology played an important role in the Kabbalah; however, it was a subordinate role. The same is true in Taoist alchemy. It can certainly help if you have the knowledge, but if you don't, it should not necessarily hinder your progress.

The Twelve Simple Letters also correspond to the month of the year, a body part or organ and a physical attribute such as speech, sight, or sexual intercourse. When it is looked at in the manner I have described, the *Sepher Yetzirah* does in effect become a great grimoire. In fact its information, incorporated into the Tree of Life diagram, forms the basis of the Western Kabbalah.

In the Western Kabbalistic schools long lists of correspondences were made up for the twenty-two letters as well as the ten sephiroth, in addition to, and sometimes substituted for, those found in the *Sepher Yetzirah*. Crowley collected these in his classic work 777. Each correspondence had a place on the Tree of Life. Meditations or rituals could be composed by physical or mental manipulation of the correspondences so as to arrive at some destination on the Tree. This will be discussed in further depth in the next chapter.

As I before stated, there are no commentaries in existence that explain what the author of the *Sepher Yetzirah*, be it the patriarch Abraham or some other, originally intended the work to be. All we really have is various versions of the book itself. The commentaries that do exist generally interpret the *Sepher Yetzirah* in terms of the currently acceptable Hebraic interpretation which changed many times down through the centuries.

## The Bardon Kabbalistic System

The system set out by Franz Bardon in *The Key to the True Quabbalah*, is vastly different from any known Hebraic interpretation, yet it is similar in many ways to Taoist Yoga. Bardon sets out a complete course of training. He removes the scriptural background that is so prevalent in all other commentaries. He leaves us with a system that can be used by anyone, not just devout Jews. This is not to say that the system is easy, it is just accessible to a wider variety of people. The same could be said for Taoist Yoga, although its background is Chinese, its teachings are available to everyone.

The Bardon system is a Western Kabbalistic one. Bardon was German and his books were originally written in German. He seems to be much better known to European Kabbalists then to those in England or America. His book on Kabbalah is an intensive course of training using the letters of the alphabet as its basis. This is the German alphabet which includes letters such as Ch, Oe and Sh which do not exist as independent letters in the English alphabet. Some mirror phonetic translations of Hebrew letters such as Cheth and Shin (Ch and Sh). However, there are obvious accretions to the system, if it is in fact based on ancient *Sepher Yetzirah* sources.

For instance, color plays a major part in Bardon's system. Each letter is assigned a color in the first step of the practice. Yet the *Sepher Yetzirah* never mentions color. However Aryeh Kaplan states at page 174 of his *Sefer Yetzirah* that a tradition of color for the planets and the sephiroth can be found in *The*

*Zohar* that follows the order found in one version of the *Sepher Yetzirah*. Hebrew Kabbalists often meditated on the color assigned to the sephiroth. Exactly when the colors were assigned to each letter is unknown. Color is a most obvious connection and being able to visualize a letter in a particular color is an excellent meditational device. All the Western Kabbalistic schools had color correspondences for the letters and the sephiroth. It is a basic tool for building a meditation or ritual.

The Taoists assigned colors to the five elements and in turn to the internal organs. The Taoist universe contained colors for the Earth, the planets and the stars. On the whole, though, color is less important to the Taoists or the Hebrew Kabbalists, where it functions more as an aid to practice, than it is to the Western Kabbalist where its function is essential.

In Bardon's system the practitioner first learns to assign colors to the individual letters of the alphabet, for instance A is light blue, B is light violet, and C is red. A series of four different exercises with the color and the letter are performed. First the student learns to "see" the color in his whole body. Next each letter is assigned to one of the four elements. Mirroring the *Sepher Yetzirah* and the Three Mother Letters, those letters assigned to the fire element are visualized in the head, those assigned to air are visualized in the chest, and those to water in the abdomen. Bardon works with the earth element as the fourth element. Letters assigned to earth are practiced from the coccyx (tail bone) down to the soles of the feet.

The next series of exercises assigns each letter and color to a particular body part. These in large part follow the correspondences in the short version of the *Sepher Yetzirah*. All of these exercises use the visualizing abilities of the student.

Next the student learns to "pronounce" the letters. Each letter is sounded at a particular note on the music scale. So that A is sounded in the pitch of note G, B in note A, C in note D, and so on. Basically the exercise proceeds so that the student combines both the sound of the letter and the color and repeats the previous exercise of hearing the note and seeing the color of each letter in 1) his whole body, 2) in its proper elemental region (head, chest, abdomen, or legs), and 3) in its corresponding organ.

The third step in Bardon's Kabbalistic training begins with learning to associate each letter with a certain feeling. This is based on its elemental correspondence. Thus, the letter A, which corresponds with the air element, is experienced as a feeling of ease or lightness. The letter B, which corresponds with the earth element, is experienced as a feeling of weight. Likewise, a letter that corresponds with the fire element would be experienced as a feeling of warmth and a water element letter with a feeling of chill. Once this is learned, the student now combines all the exercises and simultaneously sees the letter's color, hears it at its correct pitch, and feels it at its proper element (heat, chill, weightiness, or lightness). Bardon calls this Tri-polar or Tri-elemental pronunciation. It is not until this Tri-polar pronunciation is mastered that the student is able to actually use the letters creatively (as a Kabbalist).

Obviously, Bardon's system is very complex. The training outlined above actually revolves around the Three Mother Elements. All visualizing exercises are within the province of the Fire element, all auditory exercises are subject to the Air element and the feeling exercises are subject to the Water element. In effect, almost the entire course of study is based on the elements. Bardon has one short chapter on the principles of the ten sephiroth, but there are no exercises given specifically for them.

Once a student has reached the point where he can use any letter in a tri-polar manner, he no longer is a student but has truly become a Kabbalist. He is literally a force of nature, he can control the elements and the letters that God used to create and form the universe. He is the Master of the Word. The *Sepher Yetzirah* has been translated as either the *Book of Formation* or *The Book of Creation*. Bardon gives us a method to apply these terms literally so that the *Sepher Yetzirah* is seen not as some ancient philosophy, but as a vibrant system of true creative knowledge.

Unfortunately, Franz Bardon died before he could write a planned book on alchemy. As he would have said, it was the Will of Divine Providence. Few Western Kabbalists have ever heard of him. But, more than anyone else I have ever encountered, he provided a true bridge between the Hebrew and Western Kabbalah and Taoist Yoga.

~

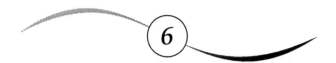

# The Tao and the Tree

The heart of the Western Kabbalah is the Tree of Life. In the chapter on the Structure of the Universe, I outlined the ten sephiroth, or vessels, which contain the emanations from the *Ein Soph*. These ten sephiroth along with the twenty-two Hebrew letters make up the thirty-two paths of the Tree of Life.

The original source of the thirty-two paths is the opening section of the Sepher Yetzirah: (Chap. 1, Sec. I):

> In thirty-two mystical paths of wisdom
> did Yah, the Lord of Hosts, the God of
> Israel, the living God, King of the
> Universe, El Shaddai, merciful and
> gracious, most high and exalted,
> Dwelling in eternity, Whose name is
> Holy, most lofty and holy—
> create the Universe with numbers,
> letters and sound.

(Sec. II):
Ten sephiroth out of nothingness
Twenty-two are the letters, the
foundation of all things."

Basically, the work of the Western Kabbalist is to learn
and master these thirty-two paths. As a system, the ten sephiroth are the basic building blocks with the twenty-two letters
forming paths connecting them. The Kabbalist moves along
these twenty-two paths to travel from sephirah to sephirah.

There are different versions of these pathways developed
by different groups and authors, but the most commonly
accepted version developed by the Golden Dawn looks like
Figure 23.

## The Golden Dawn

The information contained in this diagram forms the basis of
Western Kabbalism. In modern times, it was the late nine-
teenth-century mystical organization, the Golden Dawn, that
first taught its initiates about this Tree of Life. The founders of
the Golden Dawn claim to have gotten their information from
Germany via German manuscripts purchased second-hand in
a bookshop in England. In any case, the information was
guarded with utmost secrecy and new members of the Golden
Dawn were sworn to strict oaths of silence. This silence was
broken in 1909 when a former member of the group, Aleister
Crowley, began publishing the Golden Dawn's secrets in his
bi-annual publication *The Equinox*. In 1910 Crowley was sued
by MacGregor Mathers, the Golden Dawn's leader, to prevent
any further publication of the group's secrets. The English
judges refused to recognize any right to protect this "non-
sense" and dismissed the case. Crowley continued to publish

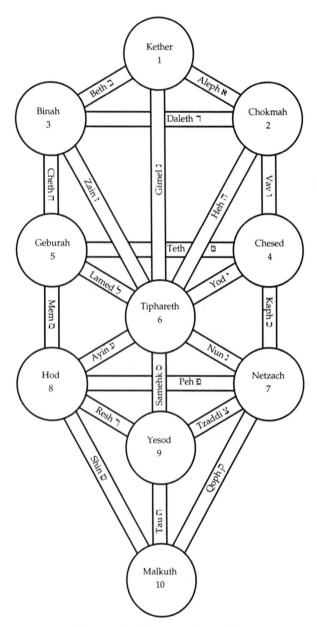

Figure 23: Kabbalistic Tree of Life

and eventually in 1937 his one-time secretary Israel Regardie published the entire curriculum of the Golden Dawn in a monumental work entitled, with no great surprise, *The Golden Dawn*.

Most modern Western Kabbalah is derived from the work of these oft-time misguided pioneers, Franz Bardon being a notable exception.

The Golden Dawn was a fraternal type organization. A new member would move up the ranks by mastering the required teachings and techniques of each grade. Membership was by invitation only. He or she would start as a Neophyte with no grade. The grades were based on the ten sephiroth. As a member progressed, he would "climb" the Tree. The first grade Zelator reflected mastery of the lowest sephiroth Malkuth, the next grade mastery of Yesod then Hod, Netzach and so on up to Kether.

I won't go into a detailed description of all the grades; that would take an entire book, and that book has already been written by Mr. Regardie. Rather, I shall describe some of the more important aspects and show their correlation to Taoist Yoga.

## The Training of a Western Kabbalist

A Neophyte would first learn about the elements, the Hebrew letters, and the signs of the Zodiac. As he progressed he would learn of the sephiroth and the paths connecting them. Many correspondences for the Hebrew letters and sephiroth would be learned. Much of the group work of the Golden Dawn was done by ritual, so he would learn the rituals of each grade. He would study the Tarot. Each of the twenty-two cards of the major arcana corresponds to a Hebrew letter, which in turn corresponds to one of the paths connecting the sephiroth. The basic principles of alchemy, the planets, metals, God and Archangel names were also mastered.

To those not familiar with Western Kabbalism, this may all sound quite confusing, so an example is certainly in order.

## Pathworking

What exactly is meant by travelling a path? It is not the same as being initiated into a grade in the Golden Dawn. This required great ritual, costumes, props, etc. Stripped of these trappings, the work can be done alone. What is attempting to be done here is a change of consciousness. The method is usually solo or guided meditations with a little ritual sometimes thrown in for good measure.

So, for instance, how would we travel from Malkuth, the tenth and "lowest" sephirah, to Yesod, the ninth sephirah? The path from Malkuth to Yesod is the thirty-second path. The thirty-second path has many correspondences that the traveller can use to guide him on his journey. It is very similar to the shamanic journey described in the first chapter. Malkuth symbolizes the Earth, Yesod is the Moon. The path typically would begin by descending into the Earth, the Lower World. Yesod is the realm of the subconscious and sexuality symbolized by the Moon. The traveller descends to find what is hidden there. The most convenient way to begin the journey would be to meditate on the Tarot card assigned to the thirty-second path and use this as a gateway. This is the Tarot card generally called the World. In most versions of this card, we see a woman encircled by the twelve signs of the Zodiac and in each of the four corners of the card is a different animal symbolizing the four elements; fire, water, air, and earth.

Meditating on the card should set off different trains of thought, be it about the Zodiac, the elements, or the woman. Yesod is the realm of the lower astral plane which is simply the realm of imagination as opposed to the upper astral which requires actual out-of-body travelling. A successful journey along the thirty-second path should free the traveller of the shackles of the earth and leave him or her free to imaginatively explore the realms of the unconscious. At the end of the journey, the traveller should feel light and gentle and refreshed.

Each path and each Tarot card symbolizes a different aspect of the Kabbalist's journey from darkness into light. The Kabbalist's ascent up the Tree of Life should be orderly. Each path must be mastered in order. The higher he climbs the more mystical the symbolism becomes. All aspects of the personality must be balanced out. The dark side of his nature must be overcome. The dual nature of sexuality must be assimilated, for each of us has a masculine and feminine nature within us. Ultimately, the goal is union with the God-head—Kether, which to a Taoist would be the same as merging with the *Tai Chi* where all exists in a state as yet undivided into male or female, *yang* or *yin*, positive or negative.

The structure of Western Kabbalism is quite different from Taoist Yoga. There is more dogma, more correspondences and ritual, but the end results are often quite consistent. At the higher levels, the two systems are virtually interchangeable.

There are many Kabbalistic practices that are quite similar to Taoist Yoga. Early in the practice, relaxation techniques are learned. Just as in the Taoist Inner Smile exercises, various internal organs and body parts are visualized and relaxed through the use of concentration and the active use of the imagination.

The Western Kabbalist has a whole battery of internal energy exercises that rival anything in Taoist Yoga. Aside from using the Tree of Life for mentally travelling the paths, techniques for visualizing the thirty-two paths within the body were developed. Energy, in the form of light or whirling balls of light are moved up and down the paths.

## The Middle Pillar Exercise

The most basic of these techniques is the Middle Pillar exercise. The Middle Pillar (see Figure 24) runs up the middle of

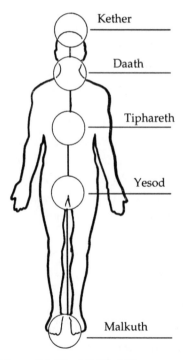

Kether

Daath

Tiphareth

Yesod

Malkuth

**Figure 24: The Middle Pillar**

the body. It is quite similar to the Thrusting Route which is taught in Fusion II, described earlier in this book.

The Middle Pillar connects the sephiroth that run down the center of the body; Kether, Tiphareth, Yesod and Malkuth.

In addition, at the level of the throat is the non-sephirah, Daath, that is also used in the exercise. In Kabbalistic philosophy, Daath separates the three upper divine sephiroth, Kether, Chokmah and Binah, from the lower seven sephiroth. This separation was known as the Abyss. Daath, which means knowledge, exists within the Abyss. It represents the knowledge of experience acquired by the Kabbalist over years of practice that is required to cross the Abyss. However, for the purpose of energy work, we are not dealing with a spiritual Abyss, only locations on the body, so this need not concern us.

The exercise combines visualizing the sephiroth as balls of light about six inches in diameter and pronouncing or more correctly vibrating the God-name appropriate to each sephirah.

We begin by picturing a brilliant ball of light at the top of the head. This is Kether. As we concentrate on it, it grows stronger and glows brighter. We now vibrate the God-name for Kether, Eheieh (pronounced "eh-hey-yeh"), sounding out each syllable slowly and rhythmically. With practice, the name is vibrated so that it is concentrated directly in the sephirah itself. It is pronounced in a low almost humming sound. Eventually, it can be done subvocally so that there is no actual external sound. This part of the exercise closely mirrors the Six Healing Sounds of Taoist Yoga in design and import. The primary difference being that the God-names are vibrated in the sephiroth while the Six Healing Sounds are vibrated in specific organs.

After a few minutes concentration on Kether, during which the divine name Eheieh is repeated a number of times, we visualize a shaft of light moving down the middle of the head until it reaches the throat. Here, at Daath, we visualize a ball of glowing light that expands to fill the entire neck region from top to bottom, front to back. Vibrate the name Yod He Vav He Elohim (El-lo-heem) several times.

Then, in similar fashion, we move the glowing shaft of light down the chest and form a ball of light in the region of the heart and solar plexus. This is Tiphareth. The name vibrated here is Yod He Vav He Eloah Va Daath ("El-oh-ah Va Dah-ot").

After a few minutes, the shaft of light descends to the region of the genitals and a ball of light is visualized there. The God-name is Shaddai El Chai (pronounced "Shad-eye El-cheye.".The "ch" is pronounced with a guttural sound as in Loch Ness and the "eye" as in the visual organ).

Finally, the shaft of light descends to the feet where a ball of light is formed and the divine name Adonay Ha Aretz (pronounced "Ah-don-eye Ha-ah-retz") is vibrated.

This is the Middle Pillar, but it is not the end of the exercise. The next phase involves circulating energy in and around the body in exercises that are quite similar to the basic Microcosmic Orbit and the supplemental energy exercises of Fusion III.

We direct our concentration back to Kether at the top of our head and we inhale breath. As we exhale, direct the energy down the front of the head, neck, torso, abdomen, and legs to the feet. With the next inhalation of breath, the energy is raised up the back of the legs, up the spine to the top of the head. This cycle is repeated a few times.

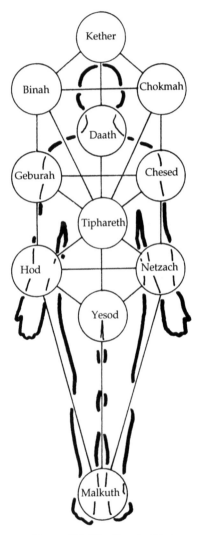

Figure 25: The Tree in Man

Next, from the top of the head, with an exhalation of breath, the energy is directed down the left side of the body to the feet. Then, with an inhalation, it is directed up the right side of the body to the top of the head.

The final part of the exercise begins by directing the concentration to the soles of the feet. With an inhalation of breath, the energy is drawn up the center of the legs, up the Middle Pillar, as if up a hollow tube. When the energy reached the top of the head, we exhale and the energy is propelled out of the top of our head and falls around us like a fountain of water. The descending energy fills in the aura around us. It is gathered back into the feet for another round with an inhalation of breath.

The Middle Pillar exercise connects energy routes within the body as well as filling in the aura around the body. Completing the aura is stressed in Taoist Yoga as well, beginning with the Fusion exercises. The aura is an energy field that surrounds the body. Usually, it is pictured as egg-shaped. It functions to seal the body's energy fields from leakage and to protect it from external negative energy.

The Western Kabbalist will continue to learn to open energy routes in the body based on the Tree of Life diagram. He is, in effect, building or growing a Tree of Life within himself (see Figure 25).

## *The Lightning Flash and the Serpent's Path*

A simple exercise for moving energy quickly down the Tree is the Lightning Flash. In this exercise, the Kabbalist imagines energy in the form of a bolt of lightning manifest from out of Nothingness (*Ayin*) and enter the top of the head at Kether.

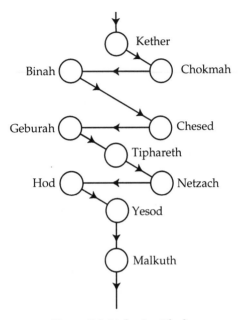

**Figure 26: Lightning Flash**

From there it quickly travels to the remaining sephiroth, down to Chokmah on the right side of the head, across to Binah on the left side of the head. Then, down and across the body to Chesed at the right shoulder and across to Geburah at the left shoulder. Next, down to Tiphareth at the solar plexus-heart region, down to Netzach at the right hip, across to Hod at the left hip, down to Yesod at the level of the genitals and, finally, straight down to Malkuth at the feet. This is an excellent exercise for grounding energy. It can be done in reverse from Malkuth upward to Kether. When it is performed upward, it is known as the Serpent's Path.

The source for these exercises are found in Chapter 1, Section 6 of the *The Sepher Yetzirah*:

The ten sephiroth out of ayin [nothing]
have the appearance of the lightning flash.
Their origin is unseen and no end is perceptible.
The word is in them as they rush forth and as
they return.

In the Serpent's Path, the energy flows upward more slowly than in the Lightning Flash and seems to encircle the sephiroth as it passes them rather than shoot right through them.

With these two exercises, we are learning to draw energy from above and below and move it through the body. In Taoist Yoga, we learn similar exercises in the Fusion practices. These types of exercises become crucial in the Kan and Li formulas especially in the Greater and Greatest Enlightenment formulas. In these exercises, energy is spiraled down from

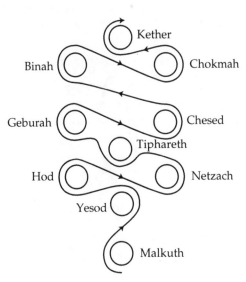

Figure 27: Serpent's Path

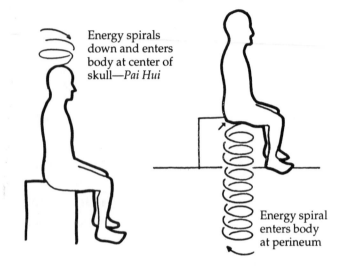

Energy spirals down and enters body at center of skull—*Pai Hui*

Energy spiral enters body at perineum

**Figure 28: Energy Spiraling from Above**

**Figure 29: Energy Spiraling from Below**

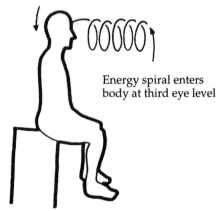

Energy spiral enters body at third eye level

**Figure 30: Energy Spiraling Horizontally**

above (the universal plane) and into the body (see Figure 28) and spiraled upward from below (the earth plane) and into the body (see Figure 29). The Taoists also spiral energy in horizontally at the point just above the bridge of the nose (the human plane) and draw this energy into the third eye (see Figure 30).

## The 32 Paths and the 32 Meridians

The great similarity between Western Kabbalism and Taoist Yoga should be more obvious now. Eventually, the Kabbalist will be able to form the entire Tree of Life in his body and connect all thirty-two paths—the ten sephiroth and twenty-two letters. He will be able to transfer his consciousness to any point on his body and consciously move energy through any or all of the thirty-two paths. You realize how close the Taoist and Kabbalistic systems really are when you become aware that in Taoist Yoga there are a total of thirty-two energy meridians in the body that we open and pass energy through. Each system has exactly thirty-two paths of energy. In the Taoist system, we learn of the Governor and Functional Channels that make up the Microcosmic Orbit. In Fusion II, we open the Thrusting Route and Belt Channels—two more meridians. In Fusion III, we learn the four Positive and Negative Arm and Leg Routes. In Lesser Enlightenment *Kan* and *Li*, we learn of the six routes that begin in each hand and each foot, twelve left side, twelve right side, for a total of twenty-four meridians. Altogether, there are thirty-two routes. The same in each system. Isn't that convenient?

## The Goals of Taoist Yoga and Western Kabbalah

It is time to stop and consider where we are going with all of this. To what end? What is the reward?

Initially, both Taoist Yoga and Western Kabbalah work on calming the mind and healing the body. To further this end in the twentieth century, many Kabbalists adopted traditional Indian Yoga techniques including stretching and postures, breathing exercises and mantra yoga (where a word or words are repeated over and over) and tantric sexual yoga. Taoist Yoga is just beginning to make an impact on this group, primarily in the area of sex, which we will discuss in the next chapter. As time goes on, I'm certain this impact will increase. Aleister Crowley, in his novel *Moonchild*, spoke of the Tao Master as being the highest adept. Crowley himself appears to have known little of the actual Taoist training. This is not surprising. Until Mantak Chia opened the door, the teachings simply were not available.

The second goal of Taoist Yoga and Western Kabbalism is balancing and harmonizing the emotions. This is learned in Taoist Fusion 1 and 2. What is actually being balanced is the elements in the body which control the emotions. The Kabbalists had numerous techniques for this. The student learns of the four elements; fire, water, air, and earth. He or she learns to visualize the fire element as a red triangle, water as a silver crescent, air as a deep blue circle, and earth as a yellow square. He or she learns exercises combining two or more elements. As shown in the last chapter on *The Sepher Yetzirah* and Franz Bardon, he learns to visualize the elements in the body, and then as the teachings become more detailed, he learns that different body parts and organs are controlled by different elements. In the Tarot, each of the four suits represents one of the elements; wands are fire, cups are water, swords are air, and disks or pentacles are earth.

The two systems mirror each other. And if we have worked hard and practiced diligently, we achieved good health in mind and body. This is ample reward for many practitioners.

But, did I hear someone out there say "I want more"? If so, then you are ready for the higher mysteries.

## The Higher Mysteries of Inner Alchemy

For some, knowledge itself is its own reward. For others, knowledge is useless unless it can be used functionally. Both Taoist Yoga and Western Kabbalism are forms of internal alchemy. Alchemy simply means to change. On a mundane level, alchemy is going on all the time. If you are feeling sad and then you see something or hear something that suddenly makes you smile and feel happy, this is alchemy. Something has changed. As we begin the practice of alchemy, being able to cause seemingly simple changes to your emotional state is a sign of success. What is to be avoided is sudden radical change which is usually an indication of severe imbalance. This is why the teachings are laborious and methodical. To reach enlightenment without first conquering the ego is what causes so many spiritual leaders and gurus to take themselves and their flock over the deep end. The best advice here is if people start telling you that you're acting crazy, listen to them carefully. They may be right.

The higher levels of Taoist Yoga and Western Kabbalah are both creative and spiritual. A Kabbalist who can pronounce a letter or series of letters in a Tri-polar manner as described in the last chapter actually controls the creative power of those letters. Don't forget the quote from the *Sepher Yetzirah* at the beginning of this chapter: "In thirty-two mystical paths of wisdom did Yah...create the universe with numbers, letters and sounds." This is serious and profound work; it is not mere idle chatter.

As to the spiritual side, the aim of Taoist Yoga is to create the Immortal Child mirrored by the Kabbalist's creation of a Body of Light. The ultimate goal is to merge this Immortal Child or Body of Light with *Wu Chi* or *Ein Soph*—Nothingness.

## *The Energy Body and the Body of Light*

The basic techniques for both systems are quite similar. An energy body is formed outside the physical body. Initially, it is done by imagination. With practice, the energy body grows stronger. Into this body the Kabbalist transfers the Tree of Life while the Taoist transfers the Microcosmic Orbit, the Thrusting Route, Belt Channels and, then, all the meridians. The Kabbalist calls this the Lower Astral Body; the Taoist calls it the Soul Body. After considerable practice, a second energy body is created above the first energy body. The Kabbalist will transfer his consciousness into this Higher Astral Body in which he can travel outside his physical body. The Taoist calls this second energy body the Spirit Body and it is again filled with the energy meridians. The Kabbalists call it the Body of Light (see Figure 31).

But, the real secret has not been revealed yet. In the Kan and Li exercises, the student of Taoist Yoga actually forms an Immortal Child within himself. This Immortal Child is carefully grown and nurtured and then transferred first into the Soul Body and then after much work into the Spirit Body. I don't want to reveal the details at this time for fear that those

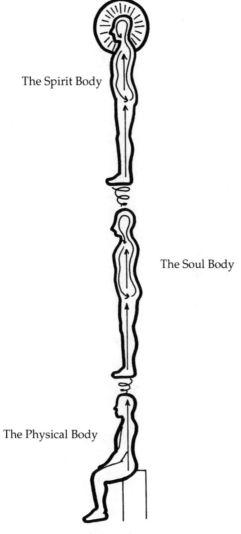

The Spirit Body

The Soul Body

The Physical Body

Figure 31: The Energy Body

unprepared would try to duplicate them. But I will give a brief description.

The process of building the energy body begins as an advanced technique of the Fusion I exercises. In the Lesser *Kan* and *Li*, drawing from energies within the body, the Soul Body is created. In Greater *Kan* and *Li*, energy is drawn from outside the body and the Spirit Body is created. As earlier stated, the basic formula of alchemy is "fire supports water." Fire energy is drawn from the heart in Lesser *Kan* and *Li*. In Greater Kan and Li, it is drawn from the Sun. In Greatest *Kan* and *Li* it is drawn from the North Star. The fire is placed below the water energy and is called the Stove. The water energy is drawn from the genital region in Lesser *Kan* and *Li* and from the earth and moon in Greater and Greatest *Kan* and *Li*. The cold water energy is raised above the stove and is visualized as being lowered into a cauldron which is heated by the stove. In Lesser *Kan* and *Li*, the cauldron is at the level of the navel (the Tan Tien). In Greater *Kan* and *Li*, it is raised to the solar plexus and in Greatest *Kan* and *Li* it is raised to the heart.

The steam generated from the boiling cauldron is drawn to the genital region and mixed with the sexual energy found there. The mixed steam and sexual energy is then raised up in the body. It is drawn to certain internal organs and the effect can only be described as having sex within the body. The process is known as Self-Intercourse and has long been one of the most closely guarded secrets of the Taoists. The organs provide a seed (the liver in Lesser *Kan* and *Li* and the spleen in Greater). In Greater *Kan* and *Li* if successfully performed, the seed is actually impregnated and a spiritual fetus is created. In Greatest *Kan* and *Li* the fetus matures and is transferred into the Spirit Body—but it is not yet mature enough to go out on its own. In the Sealing of the Five Senses, the cauldron is drawn to the brain. All the senses are sealed and complete consciousness is transferred to the immortal child.

The Western Kabbalists have somewhat similar techniques, but they are not nearly as well defined as the Taoists'. An immortal child results from a mystical marriage that takes place within the body. This immortal child is symbolized as either a fetus, a baby, or a hermaphrodite. In theory it's very similar to the Taoists, it's just surrounded with more mystical trappings. However among the Kabbalists these higher levels

Figure 32: Traveling to the Celestial Realms

are often misunderstood as symbols of various levels of Sexual Magick, which is the topic of the next chapter.

The Western Kabbalists believe that there is an immortal self within the body called the Higher Self, or the Holy Guardian Angel. To connect with this Higher Self and gain its Knowledge and conversation is called the Great Work.

The Body of Light is analogous to the Spirit Body of Taoist Yoga. The Kabbalist would transfer his consciousness to the Body of Light and travel to the upper worlds. I have found nothing in Western Kabbalism that is directly analogous to the Taoists creation of an immortal fetus although there are numerous references to becoming one with the immortal soul, creation of a child within and merging with the Godhead. These appear to be more analogous to being spiritually reborn rather than actual creation of a new entity.

Western Alchemy did in fact seek the creation of an immortal child just like the Taoists. Unfortunately, the authentic literature of Western Alchemy beyond providing a basic understanding of the concepts, is to all intents and purposes, incomprehensible. There are no authentic teachers available. As it stands today, it is much like Taoist Yoga was before Mantak Chia began publicly teaching its secrets, that is inaccessible.

～

# The Sexual Mysteries

Perhaps no areas of esoteric practices are more misunderstood then those involving sex. People who do not know or do not wish to understand equate the entire subject as evil or black magic. Images of orgies and witches sabbaths fill their mind. It is true that the sexual power can be abused, but for the most part the sexual secrets are life fulfilling, life enriching and sometimes even holy.

## The Hebrew Mysteries

The holiness of sex was especially true for the Hebrew Kabbalists. For them, sexual union was a sacred duty that joined a man and a woman into one being. It was, and still is, a holy union with God. The Jews had a whole body of teaching involving the sexual secrets. There were very definite rules concerning when, with whom, and under what circumstances union could take place. Most of these rules are found directly in *The Zohar*.

## The Zohar

For many modern Jewish Kabbalists, *The Zohar* is the Kabbalah. It is a massive multi-volume work that is in large part mystical interpretations of the Old Testament. It is very difficult reading for even a Jewish scholar. By the sixteenth century, it replaced the *Sepher Yetzirah* as the most important Kabbalistic text. As is to be expected, its authorship is shrouded in mystery. The reputed author is Rabbi Simeon Ben Yohai, a first century Kabbalist. Supposedly it was written after the Jewish uprising against the Romans in 79 A.D. Rabbi Simeon and his son were forced to flee the Romans and lived in a cave for twelve years, during which time *The Zohar* was composed. However it would appear that the actual author was a thirteenth century Kabbalist named Moses de Leon. Handwritten manuscripts of *The Zohar* first began appearing between 1280-1290 A.D. Moses de Leon, a prolific writer on his own behalf, prepared these manuscripts allegedly from the original of Rabbi Simeon Ben Yohai, which he claimed to possess. Upon his death, however, no original manuscript could be found, and both his widow and daughter claimed that Moses de Leon was the sole author. Still, there are those Kabbalists today, like the followers of Rabbi Berg, who insist that Rabbi Simeon ben Yohai wrote *The Zohar*.

Either way, *The Zohar* profoundly changed the Hebrew Kabbalah. It became much more philosophical while meditative and magical aspects began to fall into disfavor, especially after printed editions began to appear in 1558 in Mantua, Italy.

We are concerned here with what *The Zohar* had to say about sex. To understand the viewpoint of *The Zohar*, it is necessary to understand the concept of the Shekinah.

## The Shekinah

The Shekinah provides us with perhaps the most beautiful and most mystical of all the Kabbalistic doctrines. I will try my best to convey it in an intelligible form.

The Kabbalah was always the inner, esoteric tradition of Judaism. It sought to explain the outer, exoteric religion. In exoteric Judaism, the Shekinah was quite simply God's presence and relationship to the community of Israel. There is no connotation of sex or gender in this relationship.

To the Zoharic Kabbalist, the Shekinah was something quite different. The Shekinah was, is, the feminine form of God. They believed that God had both a masculine and feminine form. The Kabbalistic sexual mysteries involved union with the Shekinah—the Divine Presence on Earth.

The Shekinah had both a higher and lower nature. In her higher aspect she is the Great Mother, the womb of the Universe, Binah, the first He in God's sacred name Yod He Vav He. It is through the union of Yod and the first He that the universe is brought into manifestation. Yod is the masculine, father form of God, the provider of the seed, while the first He is the mother, provider of the egg, who gives birth to everything in existence. In Taoist terms, Yod is *Yang* and the first He is *Yin*, both in their purist forms.

In her lower form, the Shekinah is the second He in the sacred name Yod He Vav He. She is in exile on Earth as a result of the fall of man through Adam. It is the Kabbalists job to raise her, from the darkness of earthly existence, back to heaven. The Kabbalist must first get the Shekinah to come and attach herself to him. This can only be done through marriage. To the Kabbalist, marriage represents a symbolic union of God and his Shekinah. The Shekinah will not attach herself to a single man. It is also necessary that the Kabbalist have children as a result of the marriage, for this was seen as a completion of God's plan for man, and the Shekinah will not attach herself to an incomplete man.

Intercourse was to take place only once a week on the Sabbath, at midnight, for this was the moment when God was most closely united to the community of Israel. Of this *The Zohar* says: (Book I, Sec. 14a and 14b): "It is for this reason that the marital intercourse of the wise and learned men is weekly, from Sabbath to Sabbath." This wasn't as restrictive as it sounds for, generally, they spent the rest of the week away from home studying Torah and Kabbalah and only returned home for the Sabbath. Jewish Kabbalists were extremely devout people.

Intercourse had to take place face to face, with the wife between the two arms of her husband. Both partners had to be entirely naked. No intercourse could take place if the wife was menstruating.

During intercourse, the male is united to the female in a holy purpose. The union below on earth is an image of the holy union above in heaven. The unity of their being; that they are complete and unblemished; that they are one, is what the man and woman must think about during inter-course and especially at the time of orgasm.

In effect, the woman draws the Shekinah down into her-self and becomes the Shekinah, while the man firmly believes that he is having intercourse with God's Divine Presence— the Shekinah. *The Zohar* says that during intercourse the male is actually having intercourse with two females (Zohar I, Sec. 50a): "he is beatified by two females, one from the upper world and one from the lower world—the upper one to pour blessings down upon him, and the lower one to be supported by him and to be conjoined with him."

The only two exceptions to the rule on having sex only on the Sabbath night was when the husband returns from a journey away from home and after menstruation. *The Zohar* gives us a wonderful discourse on a man's journey away from home (for business or spiritual purposes) and his relationship with the Shekinah which might clarify some of the concepts here. The guiding principle is that the male must be continually attached to the female; in effect, to become male and female. This obviously doesn't mean a constant physical connection, but rather one of heart, mind, and spirit. Zohar I, Sec. 49b and 50a:

> Thereupon Rabbi Shimeon began a discourse with this text. "And he went on his journeys from the South even to Bethel, unto the place where his tent had been at the beginning, between Beth-el and Ai" (Gen. XlII, 3). He said: The word "journeys" is used here where one might have expected "journey" to indicate that the Shekinah was journeying with him. It is the duty of a man to be ever "male and female," so that his faith remain firm, and that the Shekinah never depart from him. What will you then say of a man who goes on a journey and, being away from his wife, is no longer "male and female?" The husband's remedy is to pray to God before he begins his journey, while he is still "male and female," and thus draw to himself the presence of his Master. After he has offered his prayer and thanksgiving and the Shekinah rests upon him, then he may leave, for by his union with the Shekinah he has become "male and female" as he journeys in the country as he was "male and female" in his town, as it is written: "Righteousness shall precede him and place his footsteps on the way" (Psalms 85, 14). Pay attention to this. When a man is travelling he should be most careful of his actions, so that his celestial partner will not desert

him and leave him deficient, through lack of union with
the female. If this was necessary when he was with his
wife, how much more is it necessary when a heavenly
partner has attached herself to him. When he again
reaches home, it is his duty to pleasure his wife, because
it is she who procured for him this heavenly partner.
There are two reasons for this obligation. One is that
this pleasure is a religious pleasure, and the other that it
gives joy to the Shekinah also, and what is more, by its
means he spreads peace in the world, as it is written,
"you shall find that your tent is in peace, and you shall
visit your house and not sin" (Job 5:24). (Is it a sin, one
may ask, if he does not visit his wife? The answer is that
it is a sin because he takes away from the honor of the
celestial partner who was joined with him on his wife's
account). Also if his wife becomes pregnant, the celestial partner grants a holy soul to the child, and this
covenant is called the Covenant of the Holy One,
blessed be he. He should therefore be as diligent to
obtain this gladness as to procure the gladness of the
Sabbath, which is the partner of the sages. Therefore
"you shall know that your tent is in peace," since the
Shekinah comes with you and dwells in your house, and
therefore "you shall visit your house and not sin" by
happily performing the religious duty of marital intercourse in the presence of the Shekinah. Thus the students of the Torah who separate from their wives
during the six days of the week in order to devote
themselves to study are accompanied by a heavenly
partner so that they can continue to be "male and
female." When Sabbath comes, they shall pleasure their
wives for the sake of the honor of the heavenly partner,
and to seek to carry out the will of their Master, as has
been said. Similarly, if a man's wife is observing the
days of her menstruation, during all those days that he
waits for her the heavenly partner is with him, so that
he is still "male and female." When his wife is purified,

it is his duty to pleasure her through the joyful perfor-
mance of a religious obligation. For all the reasons we
have mentioned above also apply to this case. The esoteric doctrine is that men of true faith should concentrate and put their whole thought and purpose on the
Shekinah. One may object that based on what has been
said, a man enjoys greater dignity when he is on a journey then when he is home, on account of the heavenly
partner who then travels with him. But this is not so.
For when a man is home, his wife is the foundation of
his house, for it is on her account that the Shekinah
does not depart from the house.

For the Jewish Kabbalist sex was a sacred ritual. It is
unfortunate that very few Jews are aware of the Shekinah as
the feminine form of God or that God even has a feminine
side. Judaism is so often seen as a male oriented religion. That
it is God's will to be "male and female" is unthinkable to most
practicing Jews. But it's there in *The Zohar.*

## Sexual Partners for the Western Kabbalist and the Taoist

The Western Kabbalists were much more liberal in their pro-
vision for sexual partners. Though a monogamous type relationship was often stressed, this was not an absolutely rigid
requirement.

Every man and every woman has sexual energy within
them. The quality of this energy differs in people. It is this
different quality that often leads to sexual attraction regard-
less of marital status. Sexual magicians like Aleister Crowley
made use of this energy with many partners of both sexes.
He believed that "Every man and every woman is a Star." It is
the energy radiated from stars (such as our Sun) that led to

the creation of life in our universe. Every man and woman has this star or life-force energy within them. The Taoists called it *Chi*.

It was *Jing* sexual energy that they converted into *Chi* that provided the energy to the Taoist sexual adepts of both sexes. They used sex to increase their life-force energy, not to deplete it. If done properly, it is beneficial and pleasurable to both partners. The Taoists saw that women, rather than men, were closer in spirit to the forces of nature. Their *yin*, Earth, female, sexual energy was part of an inexhaustible pool. The male adept needs to absorb this *yin* energy to balance his own energies. The female adept, in turn, needs to absorb the *yang*, heavenly, male, sexual energy to obtain equilibrium.

There are legends of male sexual vampires who could drain the life-force energy out of their female victims. There even appears to be a fear among some of Mantak Chia's female students that this is a true and legitimate fear. The truth is that it as far more likely that a male can be "vampirized" by a female adept than vice versa. The male loses energy when he ejaculates. The more he comes the more energy he loses. The female does not lose energy through orgasm, her sexual energy actually increases. It is inexhaustible. It is the female adept who will actually need multiple partners unless the man is versed in the retention of semen.

According to legend, the sexual secrets were first given to the Yellow Emperor. He was the last of the Three August Ones, the founders of Chinese civilization (the other two being Fu Shih, who discovered the symbols of the I Ching on the back of a tortoise and taught man to breed animals and write, and Shennong, the August One who taught man agriculture).

The Yellow Emperor was a great ruler, a philosopher and a physician. His teachings form the basis of Chinese Medicine, which at one time included knowledge of the bedroom arts. The Yellow Emperor was taught by three female sexual adepts who called themselves the Daughters of the Earth. They were the Plain Girl, the Dark Girl and the Selective Girl. Together they taught the Yellow Emperor the secrets of conserving semen, that illnesses and bodily ailments could be healed by using certain sexual positions, and that immortality could be achieved by continuous sexual intercourse with vast numbers of women in his harem. According to legend, he ruled for one hundred years then ascended to Heaven in broad daylight after having sex with twelve hundred women without once ejaculating.

Sex with multiple female partners became standard fare for many of the Tao masters. But this was in China in a different time, morality was different, the way of life was different.

Modern Taoists appear to have turned away from this thinking. John Blofeld in *Taoist Mysteries and Magic* describes a visit to a Taoist monastery in the 1930's before World War II, in which the abbot of the monastery taught him the secrets of internal alchemy. On the subject of sexual alchemy, the abbot said that while some authorities hold that frequent intercourse with many partners is the most rapid and effective method, this is not so, since a woman's vital force (*Chi*) unlike a man's, is inexhaustible, one knowledgeable female partner is sufficient.

Mantak Chia stresses monogamy, but in truth Tao Masters rarely impose their beliefs on other people. He would say "so if you do it and it works for you, so do it, if it doesn't work so don't do it." Then he would smile, wrinkle up his nose and squint his eyes, totally non-judgmental.

In *The Nei Pien*, a fourth century classic, Ko Hung compares sexual intercourse with fire and water, either of which can give man life or kill him, depending on his ability to control them.

On the whole though, Ko Hung believed that if the methods were known, the benefits would be proportional to the number of successive copulations. He believed that other forms of internal alchemy such as the *Kan* and *Li* practices and the ingesting of medicinal herbs were even more important in achieving success.

The most famous Taoist sexual adept was P'eng Tsu, called P'eng the Methuselah, who was reputed to have lived more than 800 years, and who claimed to have received his knowledge from Masters over 3,000 years old. In *The Secrets of the Jade Bedroom* he says that the essential part of the method is to have relations with many women while emitting semen infrequently. Taoist female adepts often had many partners as well. It was easier for a female to literally drain the life-force energy out of a man by repeated ejaculation, so great care had to be taken, unless of course this was the female's aim.

However, when a couple are both versed in the Taoist sexual secrets, there is no stronger bond between two people. "Ordinary" lovers simply will not satisfy their needs. Learning the Taoist secrets of love is one of the best things you could do for a marriage. Every woman has an inexhaustible fountain of *Chi* within her. Becoming aware of this energy and nurturing it leads to truly successful marriages.

## *Western Sexual Mysteries*

The ritual nature of sex played a major part in Western Kabbalism. Actually the Western sexual practices take two basic forms: 1) ritualistic sex and 2) sex magick.

# Ritual Sex

Ritual sex is similar in nature to that of the Hebrew Kabbalah as described above except that it is much broader in scope and is not bound by all the religious precepts of the Jews. The Western Kabbalah absorbed information and techniques from all available sources. All the Gods and Goddesses of antiquity as well as demi-gods, angels, spirits, creatures of myth, etc. are available to aid the Kabbalist in his quest. This in itself is a major divergence from Hebrew Kabbalah and is one reason why they have such little regard for Western Kabbalism. It is inconceivable to a Hebrew Kabbalist to use ancient Egyptian or Greek Gods to aid him in his spiritual growth. But this is just what the Western Kabbalist does.

Generally, ritualistic sex is used to climb the Tree of Life. The participants assume and act out the male or female roles suitable for either a particular path or sephirah. Correspondences play an important part here. For instance, to perform a ritual for the sephirah Netzach, the Kabbalist would fill the temple or bedroom with those items corresponding with Netzach, which is the seventh Sephirah. Its name translates to victory. It corresponds with the emotions, most especially love. Its planet is Venus, its most common symbols are the rose and the lamp, its color is green, its Greek Goddess is Aphrodite, and so on.

In a typical ritual the couple would invoke Aphrodite. The room would be filled with all the sights, sounds, and smells that would correspond to Netzach and thus be alluring to Aphrodite. The female partner fills her mind and body with the Goddess of Love and actually becomes Aphrodite. This is a feminine ritual, so the male imagines himself to be receiving the sexual favors directly from the Love Goddess, and thus the spell is cast and the ritual sex takes place.

Kabbalistic ritual sex is generally quite beautiful and requires absolute faith and devotion to work properly. Great care must be taken to set the proper mood, which can be quite different from that set out above, according to which path or Sephirah the couple is working with.

Another form of ritualistic sex would involve the couple listening to a previously recorded pathworking, poem, or music while making love. This requires long, slow lovemaking so that the couple enter a dreamlike state and the words or sounds then carry them off. Aleister Crowley prepared numerous works to be read during lovemaking, perhaps the most famous of these being *Atlantis*. These pieces contained more image and mood than plot and were not generally openly revealed to be works of sexual magic. That is why they often appear unintelligible. Since he lived in the days before tape recorders were available, a third person would be required to read them. He was never a prude.

Ritualized sex is obviously easily adaptable to groups. Its aim, however, should always be spiritual and never debased. Of course there are always those who will abuse this power. David Koresh may serve as an example here.

## Sex Magick

Sex Magick, as I here use the term, is more akin to the traditional concept of magic. Sex is used to power the casting of a spell. Quite simply, at the moment of orgasm, the Kabbalist concentrates on what change he wants to take place. This can be anything from mundane matters such as stopping smoking or losing weight, to affecting the health, welfare, or his relationship to other people. Sex magick can be performed alone using masturbation, heterosexually, or homosexually. It can be performed anytime, anyplace, anywhere (within reason of course). It has no divine aspects and its moral tone is only limited by the conscience of the practitioner. It is equally available to men and women.

Taoists also practiced sex magick. Here is a formula as taught by Mantak Chia in the summer of 1993, at the Teacher Training session held at Vassar College. A male and female partner engage in sexual intercourse on six consecutive days (or nights), the male does not ejaculate. On the seventh day, both partners concentrate on the desired outcome (spell) and the male does ejaculate.

Both forms of Kabbalistic sex, ritual and sex magick, owe their modern existence to Aleister Crowley. The Golden Dawn, whose secrets he ultimately betrayed, did not have any form of sexual practices. After his break with that order, he began experimenting with various forms of ritual and sex magick. Crowley was a prolific writer, but of course in the early twentieth century when sex could not be openly written about, he had to use euphemisms to describe this type of work. His writings came to the attention of an occult group in Germany, the O.T.O., which had similar sexual practices. He was invited to join and was for sometime the head of the order.

Crowley never did reveal in any explicit terms the secrets of magical sex. Until recently these secrets remained secret. A landmark publication was *A Manual of Sex Magick* by Louis T. Culling (Llewellyn Publications, 1971). Culling was the first to break the oaths of silence and bring this area to the public's attention. However, despite his claim to reveal all, there is very little of what could be called methodology in his book. Read it and reread it and you could still ask yourself—how is it done? Culling did shed some light on the Magical Child. Often referred to in the writings of Western Kabbalists, was this the equivalent of the Taoist Immortal Fetus? As it turns out, it is not. For the Kabbalists, the Magical Child is the spell itself—the "child" of magical sex between a man and a woman.

# East Meets West: Taoist Sexual Secrets and the Western Kabbalah

Up until the 1990's magical sex drew its information from traditional Western Kabbalistic sources, Sufi Mysticism (*The Perfumed Garden*), *The Kama Sutra*, and Tantric Yoga.

In 1991, two excellent and coherent books were published that broke new groundwork. One is *The Tree of Ecstacy* by Dolores Ashcroft-Nowicki (The Aquarian Press 1991). Ms. Ashcroft-Nowicki is a leading modern day English Kabbalist who hopes to break the now traditional Victorian era boundaries of Golden Dawn Kabbalism and lead in new directions. Her book is the finest I've ever seen on ritual sex magick. The other book is the rather ominously titled, *Secrets of the German Sex Magicians* by Frater U.D. (Llewellyn Publications 1991, reprinted in 1995 as *Secrets of Sex Magic*). This is probably the best book on Sex Magick available; it also throws in some ritual sex and some really weird techniques like sex with a succubus or incubus. This book is absolutely essential for the serious study of sexual magic.

Aside from being readable, and giving excellent instructions and advice, both books make extensive use of Mantak Chia's Taoist sexual secrets. So it has finally begun to happen. The Western Kabbalah has begun to absorb Taoist Yoga. While neither author appears to know much beyond the first level of Taoist teaching, its impact on both authors is startling. I don't know if either author has ever actually studied with Mantak Chia. They seem to draw their knowledge from three of Chia's books, his first book about the Microcosmic Orbit and his two volumes on the Taoist secrets of love.

Frater U.D. actually places the Microcosmic Orbit (he calls it the Lesser Energy Orbit) at the heart of his system. At pages 67-68 of his book he states: "The Lesser Energy Orbit harmonizes the sexual magis (energy) like no other exercise, making it absolutely essential if you are really serious about your sex magic. It is beneficial in so many different ways that it would be silly to ignore it.If you want to learn about the Lesser Energy Orbit, I recommend the book *Tao Yoga* by Mantak Chia." At page 122 he further states: "The finest magical protection is to make sure you are firmly in your *Hara* (his name for the *Tan Tien* below the navel) and that your Lesser Energy Orbit is flowing strongly." In order to exchange sexual energy with a partner, Frater U.D. says that it is necessary for both partners to do the Lesser Energy Orbit both before and during sex. He also draws extensively on Chia's exercises such as Testicle and Ovarian Breathing without giving explicit credit. So many references are made to Chia's work that it would seem that almost half the book is drawn from Chia's writings. I see nothing wrong with this; as a matter of fact I'm happy to see him use this excellent material. It just makes me wonder what the German sex magicians were doing before Chia began to publish?

Dolores Ashcroft-Nowicki cites Mantak Chia's *The Taoist Secrets of Love* (2 vols.) in her bibliography without specifically mentioning them in the body of her book. She also makes extensive use of the Microcosmic Orbit (with her own little twist) and Testicle Breathing (which both she and Chia also call "the Dance of the Testes"). On pages 27-29 and again at 111-113 she describes the Microcosmic Orbit in detail. The only difference is that she has the orbit begin at the genital center and run up the front of the body to the tip of the tongue and then returning the attention to the sex center and again pulling the energy up but this time up the back over the buttocks and up the spine, over the head down the nose and in through the nostrils to the roof of the mouth. Then touch the tip of the tongue to the roof of the mouth and the two meridians unite. She uses this exercise for energy and healing and adds some additional unique touches that I'm certain she would like to share with us. Ms. Ashcroft-Nowicki adds color to the orbit for various different purposes. Western Kabbalists love color.

Using red colored light in the morning will make you feel stronger and brighter. You use blue colored light to calm yourself down, green colored light can stimulate your creativity. Yellow, gold and deep rose are used for healing and work especially well after surgery. Orange stimulates the communication centers in the throat and is thus useful to those who earn a living by speaking or writing. Violet and indigo are used before going to sleep and can help stimulate dreaming for a purpose such as untangling problems. Ms. Ashcroft-Nowicki suggests that violet and indigo can also be used by a dying initiate to help to cleanly and quickly release the silver cord that connects the initiate to life.

It is quite satisfying to see how quickly the Western Kabbalists have taken to Taoist Yoga and made it their own. As more information becomes available this trend is bound to continue. The full import of Taoist Alchemy is staggering.

## Testicle and Ovarian Breathing Explained

As briefly mentioned in the chapter on Taoist Yoga, aside from the Microcosmic Orbit, which is not necessarily a sexual exercise, the first sexual exercise a student learns is called Testicle Breathing for men and Ovarian Breathing for women. It is a simple and gentle exercise and is basically the same for both sexes.

Sitting near the edge of a seat, the man puts his awareness on his testicles; the woman puts her awareness on her ovaries. Taking a deep but gentle breath, the man uses his mind and slight muscular contraction to lift up the testicles. The woman slightly contracts the vagina while pulling the ovaries' energy down to the perineum. When the sexual energy begins to increase, it is slowly led up to the coccyx and step by step up the sacrum, spine and neck and into the head. This procedure is done nine times, filling the brain with sexual energy. Men then spiral this energy nine times clockwise, then nine times counter-clockwise in the head. Women spiral this energy in a reverse pattern, nine times counter-clockwise and then nine times clockwise. Men can leave the energy in the head. Women must bring the energy down the front Microcosmic channel because it is too hot to leave in the head and then store it in the navel. This exercise strengthens the entire pelvic area and brings revitalizing sexual energy (*jing*) up to the brain as well as strengthening the flow of energy in the Microcosmic Orbit.

## The Big Draw

The Big Draw also known as the Power Lock for men and Orgasmic Upward Draw for women is a powerful technique for drawing aroused sexual energy up to the higher centers of the body, thereby transforming it into life-force and spiritual energy. These methods are used in both single and dual cultivation, which means that they can be practiced with or without a sexual partner. This exercise is especially important for men because it begins the process of learning to control ejaculation. In Taoist theory, man loses a tremendous amount of energy when he ejaculates. This accounts for why men generally feel tired after orgasm. By learning to control orgasm, he can retain rather than lose this energy. Practice leads to the ability to actually having an orgasm without ejaculating. Women do not lose energy during orgasm. They can experience multiple orgasms and actually feel energized. This is why the Taoists say that man's sexual energy is limited while the woman's sexual energy is unlimited. Women do lose sexual energy during menstruation, however.

Again, the exercise is basically similar for men and women. It is necessary that, whether you are doing this alone or with a partner, you be sexually aroused before starting the exercise. For the man, he must begin before he reaches orgasm. Once it starts, it's too late.

Begin by inhaling a short sip of air, then push the tongue up to the roof of the mouth and clench the teeth. Pull the chin inward toward the back of the neck, contract the muscles in the eyes and look upward toward the crown. Contract the anus and pull up the genitals, perineum and the buttocks. This activates the sacral pump which sends energy up the spine. Clench the fists, arms and legs. Keep the shoulders and chest relaxed. While this all sounds complicated, when it is done, it all happens just about simultaneously. Sexual energy is then drawn up the spine and into the head. It is spiralled there in the same manner as in Testicle/Ovarian Breathing. In this exercise, the man must draw the energy down to the navel, because it is too hot to be stored in the head. Women can leave this energy in the head.

These are the basic Taoist sexual exercises. There is a great deal of teaching on dual cultivation (sex with a partner).

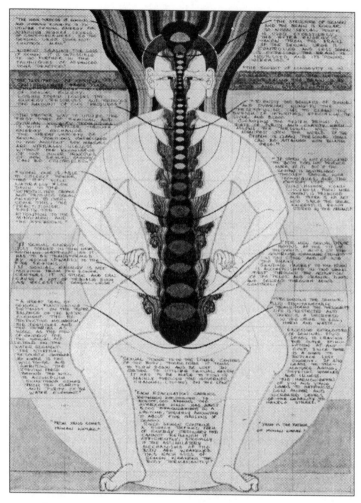

Figure 33: Seminal Kung Fu as taught by Mantak Chia

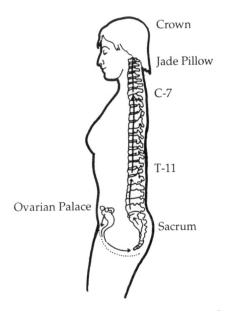

Crown

Jade Pillow

C-7

T-11

Ovarian Palace

Sacrum

**Figure 34: Cultivating Female Sexual Energy/Orgasmic Upward Draw**

At a very basic level, a couple's sex life is tremendously boosted by the exercises. There are techniques also that extend a man's staying power so that sex can sometimes go on for hours. There are techniques for whole body orgasms. Sexual positions are taught to promote healing and energy flow. There are unique exercises for men using weights and for women using a jade egg (and weights, if desired) to increase the strength of the sexual organs and the tendons.

However, it is in the *Kan* and *Li* exercises that the Taoists took the sexual secrets to new heights. This was discussed in the last chapter. During the Kan and Li Enlightenment exercises, the sexual energy is converted into a new type of energy that actually revitalizes the mind and body. This was part of the true alchemical process. Self-intercourse is a sexual secret that is found nowhere else in sexual literature. This is the greatest sexual secret, to actually experience the male and female energy within the body engage in sexual intercourse. Ultimately, this can be experienced outside the physical body in the immortal spirit body.

The Taoists were well aware of sex magick as used by the Western Kabbalists. They took it one step further. Using self-intercourse, the magical spells they could cast were peerless.

The wealth of sexual knowledge gathered up by the Taoists over the centuries was enormous. I have just touched

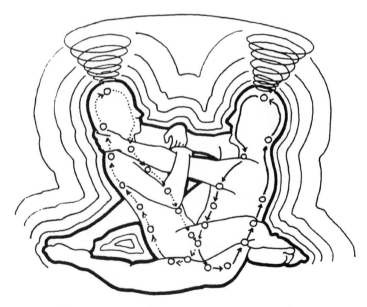

Figure 35: *Yin* and *Yang* Sexual Energy Exchange

on some of it here. At its higher levels, it far surpasses any other known sexual system in scope and imagination. We are lucky to live in an age where this information has become available.

# The North Star
# and Teli

I have been fortunate for a number of years now to have lived just a few miles from Mantak Chia's home. Over the years we have remained good friends and I was provided with the opportunity to learn and explore the very highest formulas of Taoist Internal Alchemy. Chia has never publicly taught some of these advanced formulas. So much of what I write here will be new to even his long time students.

Again, these advanced formulas find a remarkable correlation in the *Sepher Yetzirah* and the work of Franz Bardon and even Aleister Crowley. It is with great humility that I even attempt to put this information down in writing.

Mantak Chia encouraged me to write this book and bring his teachings to students of the Kabbalah. I note with personal sadness his moving back to his native Thailand to establish a permanent Taoist Retreat Center in Chiang Mai. I will miss him. I look forward to the day, sometime in the future that I will again be able to spend time with him.

## The Intermediate Formulas: Kan and Li

Taoist Yoga as taught by Mantak Chia is an orderly system that builds upon itself as the student progresses. It cannot be learned overnight and takes many years to work up to the highest levels.

There are many reasons for this to be so. On one level it is a weeding out process. Those not capable or worthy of receiving and understanding the higher levels will drop out and no longer pursue the study. Also the body goes through a series of internal changes that take some time to absorb and adjust to. These changes can be quite profound and awe inspiring. They can also be frightening. It is important to have a teacher available to guide you through the intricacies of higher internal alchemy. This is why I was so lucky to have Mantak Chia nearby. He now teaches the more advanced levels, beginning with Lesser *Kan* and *Li*, only in Thailand where he and other advanced teachers are available to give guidance.

The lower formulas such as the Microcosmic Orbit and the Fusion of the Five Elements do not require the same type of personal attention. They can safely be practiced by anyone, anywhere. Even Lesser *Kan* and *Li* is relatively safe. Beginning with the Greater *Kan* and *Li* formula, careful monitoring of the student's progress is really required. These formulas are often referred to as the Lesser, Greater and Greatest Enlightenments.

In Lesser *Kan* and *Li* the stove and cauldron are established in the lower *Tan Tien*, behind and slightly below the navel. At this level, we are only working with energies that exist within the body. the Fire energy is drawn from the adrenal glands and the heart. The Water energy is drawn from the kidneys and the sexual organs. As previously mentioned, the location of the Fire and the Water energies are inverted. Fire is drawn below to the stove, a cauldron is visualized, and Water energy is raised above and deposited in the cauldron, where it is heated by the stove and begins to steam. This is the basic formula; there are about twelve sub-formulas.

A *Kan* and *Li* session should be preceded by doing the Fusion exercise wherein the five elements are gathered together in the *Pa Qua* behind the navel, harmonized and then moved through the Creation cycle to transform negative emotions into positive emotions. This is followed by clearing the Thrusting Routes which travel up and down the center of the body and the Belt Routes which travel around the body, the main Belt Route circles the body at the navel level. This should be done in the morning at least two hours before the Lesser *Kan* and *Li* exercise.

Some of the twelve sub-formulas include steaming the glands and organs, steaming and increasing the pulses, steaming the lymphatic system, opening twelve additional channels (acupuncture meridians), creating the inner eye, steaming the thymus, pituitary and pineal gland, self-intercourse and steaming the spine and nervous system.

The Lesser Kan and Li is concluded by collecting the refined energy at the Tan Tien below the navel. The two eyes are used to "turn the wheel." The eyes are first rolled down toward the perineum. They direct energy into the Microcosmic Orbit. The eye muscles are then pulled in slightly and the genitals are pulled up as the eyesight turns inward and upward and directs the *Chi* up the spine and into the brain. This was also called the Backward Flowing Method. It is as if you were rolling your eyes 360 degrees. Although this is of course a physical impossibility, you actively imagine that this is exactly what is happening. With a little practice you get it. With each rotation, the refined *Chi* is poured into the Cauldron behind the navel as it moves downward.

In the Greater *Kan* and *Li*, the cauldron is moved upward, from the *Tan Tien* behind the navel, to the *Tan Tien* at the level of the solar plexus. This creates a more powerful steaming agent. We begin to work with external energies at this level. The energies of the Sun are combined with the adrenal and heart energy to provide the Fire for the stove. Moon energy is combined with kidney and sexual energy to provide the Water to fill the Cauldron. Cold Water energy is raised to the level of the heart and lowered into the cauldron, while hot Fire energy is lowered to the navel *Tan Tien* and then raised to the solar plexus region just below the cauldron. The temperature in the cauldron is controlled by "seasoning" it with cool energy drawn from the lungs (the White Tiger) or warm energy drawn from the liver (the Green Dragon) to keep it from getting too hot or too cold.

The Pearl is strengthened and can be projected down into the Earth to contact or interact with animal, plant, flower and tree energies. This is clearly derived from the shamanic practices described earlier in this book.

Self-intercourse in this formula is concerned with creating a spirit body. Energy is drawn from the pineal gland and mixed in the solar plexus *Tan Tien* with sexual energy drawn from the genitals. This creates an ecstatic feeling within the body. The seed (sperm) is drawn from the spleen into the cauldron. If properly done, it results in the pregnancy of the spirit body. We are here moving into some of the greatest mysteries of Taoist Internal Alchemy. I will not reveal the entire formula because it should not be practiced until the student has mastered the previous levels. It is at this point in the practice that the presence of an experienced teacher is really necessary.

The spirit body can be sent into the upper worlds to travel where it wills or to meet spirit guides. Again, pure shamanism.

Once a pregnancy takes place, all steaming practices should be stopped. This is truly a transforming experience and can be quite uncomfortable at times.

A Greatest *Kan* and *Li* session ends with rolling of the eyes as described above, except this time the energy is collected in the cauldron at the solar plexus. The Greatest *Kan* and *Li* can be performed in the morning directly after doing the Fusion of the Five Elements.

## The Planets and the Stars

Taoist Yoga seeks to connect the practitioner with not only the forces of nature on the Earth, but with extraterrestrial forces as well. The Sun and Moon, as described above, and the planets and the stars.

Although originally reserved for only his most advanced students, Chia now teaches contacting and drawing in energy from the Big Dipper(Ursa Major) and the North Star(Polaris) as advanced levels of the Microcosmic Orbit. In advanced formulas of the Fusion of the Five Elements, we connect with the *Chi* of the planets, which in turn enrich the *Chi* of the associated organs. Jupiter corresponds with Wood and the liver, Mars with Fire and the heart, Saturn with Earth and the spleen, Venus with Metal and the lungs and Mercury with Water and the kidneys. Each planet also corresponds to the appropriate color for the planet. Its energy is experienced as snow falling from above. Blue snow for Mercury, red snow for Mars, green snow for Jupiter, white snow for Venus and yellow snow for Saturn (in all due respect to the late Frank Zappa, you can eat this yellow snow). The complete formulas are available in Chia's book *Fusion of the Five Elements I.*

# *The North Star and the Big Dipper*

The Taoists believe that life on Earth was seeded by organic and inorganic particles and forces originating in the universe. We are not necessarily talking aliens here. The seeds of life could have arrived from comets, meteors, solar and stellar winds, supernovas, cosmic rays, etc. Many scientists hold similar beliefs.

To the Taoists this was known collectively as Heavenly *Chi*. In simple terms we are dealing with the *Chi* of the Sun, Moon, planets, and stars.

In the advanced practices, the *Chi* of the Seven stars of the Big Dipper and the North Star are of crucial importance. As the practitioner advances this star Chi becomes more and more important.

The energy of the Big Dipper is experienced as vibrant red light. The North Star Polaris is experienced as violet light. In the Microcosmic Orbit and Fusion of the Five Elements, first the red light of the Big Dipper is brought into the brain. Next, the stars of the Big Dipper are aligned to wrap around the lower half of the body. Imagine that the star at the tip of the handle of the Big Dipper, Alkaid, shines its red light in your solar plexus. The next star on the handle is Mizar; it shines behind your navel. The third star, Alioth, shines at the Sexual Palace at the base or root of the sexual organ. Megrez shines its brilliant red light at your perineum. Pheeda shines at the tip of your coccyx. Merak shines in your sacrum and Dubhe shines in the Door of Life, the point on the spine directly behind the navel. The stars of the Big Dipper attract the purple light of the North Star. This is their main function. The line in the back from Merak to Dubhe draws down the purple light of the North Star, first through the crown, then down the neck and spine to the stations of the seven stars of

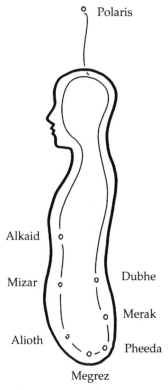

Polaris

Alkaid

Mizar

Alioth

Dubhe

Merak

Pheeda

Megrez

**Figure 36: The *Chi* of the Big Dipper**

the Big Dipper (see Figure 36). The resulting light energy can then be circulated in the Microcosmic Orbit. Mantak Chia provides a different and excellent exercise in *Awaken Healing Light of the Tao* (pgs. 414-429).

It is in the Greatest *Kan* and *Li* that this star energy becomes a crucial part of the process. The red and violet lights of the Big Dipper and Polaris are gathered below the crown and added to the Fire of the stove, providing a tremendous boost of energy.

In the Greatest *Kan* and *Li*, the cauldron is moved to the level of the heart. It is the final formula of intermediate alchemy.

In this formula, the Fire energies or stove are gathered together in the Crystal Room (or Crystal Palace), beneath the crown. The Crystal Room comprises that area in the brain which includes the pituitary, pineal and thalamus glands. A more potent form of Water is drawn by projecting deep into the Earth and drawing cold Water energy from the Earth itself. The Fire energy is drawn down to the solar plexus and the Water energy is drawn up to the throat center. They are coupled in the cauldron in the center of the body at the level of the heart.

One interesting sub-formula involves a more advanced method of connecting with each of the seven stars of the Big Dipper. In this variation, the stars connect with various points on the skull (see Figure 37), and the North Star connects with the Crystal Room.

Starting at the end of the handle of the Big Dipper, the star Alkaid is both visualized as brilliant red light and felt as being at the top of the crown of the head. The next star Mizer is visualized and felt at the base of the skull and likewise Alioth at the bottom of the chin. The star at the inner top of the Dipper Megrez is seen and felt at the left temple, and Pheeda is experienced at the right temple. Merak is visulaized and felt at the right mastoid(top of the jaw) and Dubhe at the left mastoid.

As the stars are actually positioned in the night sky, a line drawn from Merak to Dubhe and continued straight ahead will point almost directly to Polaris. The North Star Polaris is at the tail end of the constellation known as The Little Dipper or Ursa Minor. The stars of the Big Dipper

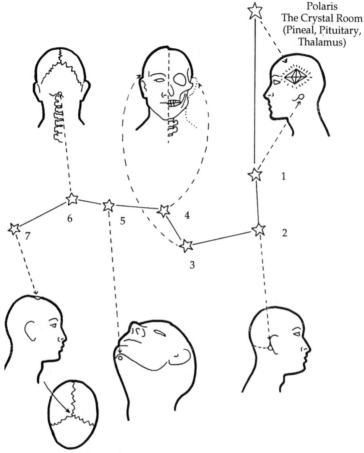

1. Dubhe; 6 A.M.; The Pivot of the Sky; Left Mastoid (Wood) Jupiter (Thursday) Near West

2. Merak; The Revolver; Right Mastoid (Water) Mercury (Wednesday)

3) Pheeda; The Rotator of the Sky; The Right Temple (Earth) Saturn (Saturday)

4. Megrez; The Leveling Light; Left Temple (Water) Mercury (Wednesday)

5. Alioth; The Balancing Light; Chin; (Fire) Mars (Tuesday) Near North

6. Mizar; The Generaing Light; Base of the Skull (Metal) Venus (Friday)

7. Alkaid; The Harmonizing Light; Crown; 6 P.M.; (Water) Mercury (Wednesday)

Figure 37: Connecting with the Big Dipper

draw the purple light of the North Star down into the Crystal Room and allow it to shine there. It then descends into the cauldron at the heart level.

Directing star energy to points of the body provides a definite, substantial feeling of something actually being there. It is not easy to describe. However its seems to be more than mere imagination.

There are other sub-formulas in the Greatest *Kan* and *Li*. Much of the work is done on opening the heart center. Also a meditation is taught to collect star *Chi* from the twenty-eight constellations. When done properly, you imagine that you have a giant body, billions of light years from head to toe. You become the Cosmic Being whose Crystal Palace is the North Star, who has constellations and planets for vital organs, whose heart is the Sun, whose kidneys are the Moon, and whose *Tan Tien* is the planet Earth. This Cosmic Being— the mind of Tao—beams down its exquisite rays to one cell of its body, you, sitting on a chair on planet Earth, meditating up on the stars.

At the end of a Greatest Kan and Li session, the refined energy is "breathed" or absorbed , directly into the bones for storage. A session can also be done in the morning after doing a short Fusion exercise.

## The Sealing of the Five Senses and the Seven Double Letters

We now approach advanced Taoist Internal Alchemy. These formulas have never been openly taught. It is when these highest levels are reached that the practitioner feels the need to leave society and retire to the mountains. The body and its functions slow down. You want peacefulness and seclusion. As a practical matter, to function in society, your daily practice would consist of lower formulas, unless you are extraordinarily gifted.

In the Sealing of the Five Senses, the *Tan Tien* is moved to the Crystal Room in the brain. It is sometimes referred to as the Heavenly Heart. There are seven openings in the skull: the left and right eyes, left and right ears, left and right nostrils, and the mouth. These seven openings represent the five senses. The mouth is separated into lips which touch, and tongue which tastes; the nose smells, the ears hear; and the eyes see. In this formula the senses are sealed in the cauldron. First connect each organ to its proper sense. The energy of the two eyes and seeing are brought to the third eye area between and slightly above the eyes. The energy of the two ears and hearing are brought to the back of the skull. They are all collected into the cauldron. Next the energy of the two nostrils and smelling, the lips and touching and the tongue and tasting are combined and also brought into the cauldron in the Crystal Palace. We visualize that out in space the cup of the Big Dipper fills with the purple light of the North Star. We visualize the Big Dipper being turned over and the purple light of Polaris is poured into the cauldron in the Crystal Room in our brain. This creates tremendous light. The light of the Tao. This is as much of the formula as I will reveal at this time.

The higher formulas really require years of practicing the lower and intermediate formulas before one is ready to perform them. It is highly recommended that anyone seeking to practice Taoist Interal Alchemy should make every effort to locate a teacher especially for all the *Kan* and *Li* and more advanced formulas. What I've given here is just the bare bones outline of the actual practice.

Now we turn to a little spiritual detective work and look for correspondences in the Kabalah. And they are there.

Chapter 4 of *Sepher Yetzirah* deals with the Seven Double Letters. Each of these seven letters corresponds with one of the seven openings to the head as found in the Sealing of the Five Senses formula. Beth(ב) is the right eye. Gimel(ג) is the left eye. Dalet(ד) is the right ear, Kaph(כ) is the left ear. Peh(פ) is the right nostril, Resh (ר)is the left nostril and Tav (ת) is the mouth.

In each system we are dealing with the same seven openings. The *Sepher Yetzirah* itself provides no instructions, but I have earlier shown the hidden alchemical tradition there.

To try to put it together requires us to better understand the significance of the North Star to this work. The North Star provides the practitioner with a celestial pole. It is the center around which everything else revolves. Once aligned with the North Star, the alchemist becomes, in effect, the center of the universe.

So where do we find this in *Sepher Yetzirah?* It's there, and again hidden. In Chapter 6 there appears what Aryeh Kaplan called one of the most mysterious words in the entire book. That word is Teli(תלי). It has generally been translated as Dragon or Celestial Dragon. Many of the ancient Hebrew sources say it refers to the constellation Draco, popularly known as the Dragon.

Draco is a northern constellation the tail of which is between the Big Dipper and Polaris. *Burnham's Celestial Handbook*, Vol.2, the Astronomer's Bible, tells us that Polaris was not always the North Star because over long periods of time the Earth's axis shifts in relationship to the sky. In the future the star Vega in the constellation Lyra will become the North Star. In 2800 B.C., the time of Abraham, the North Star was Thuban, a star in the tail of Draco!

In Abraham's time the constellation Draco served the same purpose as the Big Dipper and Polaris does in modern Taoist Alchemy. Draco wraps around the north heavens. My best guess is that ancient Hebrew students were able to use this information in a similar manner as used in the advanced Taoist alchemical formulas. The ancient Hebrew Kabbalist aligned himself with the North Star, Thuban, and used this as his celestial pole.

In the Great Pyramid at Gizah in Egypt, if one were to look upward from the tomb of the Pharaoh Khufu, you would see a small rectangular opening to the sky above. Astronomers have shown through astronomical calculations that at the time Khufu had the Pyramid built, if you looked through the rectangular hole, you would be looking directly at Thuban. Again please note that Abraham was reputed to be knowledgeable in all the mystical sciences of Egypt and alchemy translates as the Egyptian matter.

So, is this all correct? I don't really know. With the methods of Taoist alchemy available to me, it all points to a common source and makes sense out of what previously made no sense.

The actual language used in the *Sepher Yetzirah*, Chapter 6, states:

> 1. There are three Mothers and from them emanated three Fathers and their offspring. Seven are the planets and their host, Twelve are the diagonal boundaries. And the proof of this, faithful witnesses, are the universe, the year and the soul.
>
> A rule of Ten, Three, Seven and Twelve, and he appointed over them the Teli, the cycle and the heart.
>
> The Three are fire, water, and air; fire above, water below and air mediating between them. A sign of these things is that the fire supports water. Mem

hums, Shin hisses and Alef, a breath of air which places them in equilibrium.

2. The Teli in the Universe is like a king upon his throne.

   The cycle of the year like a king over his dominion.

   The heart in the soul is like a king in war.

We can see that the Teli is mentioned in the midst of the alchemical formula: the fire supports water. "The Teli (Celestial Dragon) in the universe is like a king upon his throne." Everything revolves around it, from this regal viewpoint. The analogy to the Cosmic Being whose Crystal Palace is the North Star seems appropriate. Aryeh Kaplan says that the reference to the Heart refers to the Heart of Heaven. As mentioned, another name for the Crystal Palace is the Heavenly Heart. In Western Alchemy, it was called the Philosopher's Stone.

Actually, much of this is of historical interest only. Thuban is no longer the North Star: Polaris is. If I were teaching this today, I would substitute Polaris and the Big Dipper for Draco. The cycle of the year revolves around them, the constellations of the zodiac revolve around them, the universe revolves around them, from our vantage point here on Earth.

As often mentioned, the *Sepher Yetzirah* contains mysteries within mysteries.

## Star Magick

I am uplifted in thine heart; and the kisses of the stars rain hard upon thy body." ( *The Book of the Law*, II. 62, 1904)

We have travelled now to the stars themselves and drawn their energies down into ourselves. We have drawn down the purple light from above. The true light of the North Star is purple beyond purple, purple beyond eyesight. It is the purple of the violet ray of transformation.

Purple is the color of alchemical transformation in the Western Alchemical Tradition. Purple is the seventh ray. To modern day followers of the teachings of Saint Germain, connecting with the purple light of alchemy is at the heart of the system.

To find this perfect correlation between Taoist and Western Alchemy is extraordinary. Actually, being able to experience the star energy requires diligence and practice. When I first learned of drawing star energy, it seemed almost silly. Initially it requires the active use of the imagination. But with practice it becomes more real. As you climb through the levels of alchemy, the body and mind become more attuned to sensing and experiencing subtle energies. There is a Taoist expression describing the effects of this gradual transformation: that which was real becomes false while that which was false becomes real.

A simple Taoist star energy exercise is to pick any star in the sky (it could be Polaris), and imagine that its light is spiraling down into your eyes. Do this a few times and you will find that it soon feels like more than imagination. You can feel something spiraling down: the light of the stars.

## Aleister Crowley and the Book of the Law

In the Western Kaballah, one of the great mysteries of the twentieth century is that of Aleister Crowley and *The Book of the Law*. This strange book has either delighted, baffled, or grossed out anyone who has ever read it.

Crowley claimed that on three consecutive nights: April 8, 9, and 10 in 1904, while on his honeymoon with his wife Rose in Cairo, Egypt, a new era was born for mankind. The Aeon was proclaimed. This was accomplished when Rose spontaneously announced the presence of Aiwass, a discarnate being, who referred to himself as "the Minister of Hoor-Paar-Kraat." Rose then channeled a chapter of a book on each of three consecutive nights. This short three-part book eventually became the focal point of Crowley's life. He believed it came from a higher being. It changed his life.

Whether there really was an Aiwass or merely a projection of Crowley's unconscious cannot be known.

However, this mysterious work that Crowley referred to as *The Book of the Law* or *Liber L. Vel Legis* is, in large part, concerned with star magick, "the unveiling of the company of heaven."

In Egyptian mythology, Nuit was the Goddess of the Sky. Her body contained all the planets and stars in the night sky. At the end of each day, she would swallow the sun, which would pass through her body during the night and be excreted each morning. Crowley referred to the first chapter of *The Book of the Law* as the "Book of Nuit" or "Liber Nuit." It is Nuit who proclaims "every man and every woman is a star."

In the cosmology of *The Book of the Law*, Nuit has a consort, Hadit. Nuit represents infinite space and Hadit is any point within infinite space. If you grasp the concept, it is simple. In infinite space, any point is equally in the center of that space. To become aware that you are in the center of infinity is the proper mindset. By the same token, every star in the heavens is in the center of infinite space. And as previously discussed, each person is a living embodiment of energy from the stars. Thus, every man and every woman is a star. In the words of Hadit, "In the sphere I am everywhere the center, as she (Nuit), the circumference is nowhere found." (II.3)

I don't want to explore *The Book of the Law* here in any great depth. My point is that star magick, drawing energy from the stars and identification of the self as being in the center of the universe plays an important role in modern Western Kabbalism. *The Book of the Law* has many analogies to the higher levels of Taoist Alchemy. I predict that as Western Kabbalists learn more about Taoist Yoga many of the Taoist practices will be absorbed into the Kabbalistic system.

## The Congress of Heaven and Earth

This is actually an advanced sexual formula. It involves the creation of a male (*yang*) and female (*yin*) entity within the body. They have intercourse within the brain resulting in full development of the pineal gland. The sensation is difficult to describe. It is as if the pineal gland has become the male sexual organ which is brought to orgasm by the undulations of the pituitary gland which acts as a female sexual organ, while the thalamus acts as the cauldron. The thalamus is also the gland that directly connects with the North Star.

At an even higher level, the intercourse takes place outside the physical body in the spirit body between a heavenly God and Goddess.

Franz Bardon in *Initiation into Hermetics* (between pages 16 and 17) has a wonderful full color picture of what he calls the first tarot card. Above the head of the central figure is a crown, and above the crown is a clear globe within which a heavenly man and woman are copulating. He describes this image as representing the procreative positive and negative forces which stand for the creating act of the universe. Clearly, Bardon was familiar with this formula though he never specifically refers to it anywhere else in his writings.

To a Hebrew Kabbalist, what is being described here is intercourse between the higher Shekinah (Binah) and the Great Father (Chokmah). I know of no authentic Hebrew sources that describe such practices. But then again, there really are no words that could adequately describe intercourse between the positive and negative creative forces in the universe. Remember, Chokmah consciousness is beyond the verbal powers of the intellect.

## Return to the Source

The highest light is the clear light. It is beyond the purple light.

In the Hebrew Kabbalah, it is the clear light that is unmoving and unchanging, that pervades all of creation. It is like the canvas upon which the universe is painted.

In Lurianic Kabbalism, the clear light preceded all of creation. It is the *Ein Soph Aur*, the Limitless Light. As stated, Lurianic Kabbalism is immensely complex. Luria's version of creation was stunning.

Prior to creation, the *Ein Soph* was limitless. In order to allow creation to take place, the *Ein Soph* has to create a space in which creation could take place. To accomplish this, the *Ein Soph* contracted into itself. It contracted to a single point. This is known as the *Tsimtsum*. However, despite the contraction, there remained an essence of the *Ein Soph*, a higher light that lingered in the space the *Ein Soph* had contracted from. To conceptualize this, imagine a bottle filled with wine. Pour out the wine and there will still be the aroma of the wine lingering in the bottle. Now, instead of pouring out the wine, imagine it condensing into a single point within the bottle. This is sort of like the *Tsimtsum*. The next step involved the creation of the primordial man, Adam Kadmon, at the point of concentration. From the eyes of Adam Kadmon came the emanation of light to fill each sephirah and create the universe. However, after the light from Adam Kadmon's eyes shown into Kether, Chokmah and Binah, the next sephirah Chesed was not strong enough to contain the light of original creation and it shattered. It was this shattering of the vessels that brought chaos and evil into the universe. It was necessary that a second creation take place. This time the light issued forth from the forehead of Adam Kadmon and this time the sephiroth held. But, it is the shattered sparks from the original creation that the Lurianic Kabbalist must unify and return to the *Ein Soph* to fulfill the original plan of creation.

All religions seem to have a tradition of a higher light, a light of heaven, a clear light. Kabbalistic Judaism and Taoism are no different.

Taoists call rejoining this light the Return to the Source or the Union of Heaven and Man. After intercourse between the divine man and divine woman in the Congress of Heaven and Earth, the spirit body obtains immortality and merges with the Higher Light of the Tao, the *Wu Chi*.

There are legends of Taoist Immortals who could leave their bodies on earth in a state of suspended animation and travel through space for years on end before returning to their bodies. One such recent legend tells of a detachment of Communist soldiers finding a group of non-decaying, but not apparently living bodies in a cave. The bodies were ordered burned. In time, the Taoist Immortals returned to earth only to find their bodies had been destroyed. Their methods of revenge taken against the soldiers would make for an interesting novel.

How can I describe merging with the Source, returning to Heaven? I cannot. It is the ultimate mystical experience reserved for the very few highest adepts.

Occasionally, an adept will contact or be contacted by a discarnate immortal. Both Taoists and Kabbalists tell similar stories. The great Rabbi Joseph Caro (1488-1575) was a member of the circle of mystics living in Safat, Israel in the early sixteenth century which included Isaac Luria and Moses Cordovero. Caro had a heavenly mentor called by the Kabbalists a Maggid. His Maggid taught him kabbalistic secrets. He recorded these communications in his diary. Rabbi Moses Hayyin Luzzato (1707-1746), a Lurianic Kabbalist, also claimed to have a maggid. Isaac Luria himself is reputed to have had a Maggid as well. There are numerous Taoist legends of similar experiences.

And here ends my attempt to explore the highest levels of Taoist Alchemy and the Kaballah. I hope I have been successful in at least making some of the concepts comprehensible.

~

# *Conclusion*

In this short book, I have attempted to show the similarities and differences between Jewish Kabbalism, Western Kabbalism and Taoist Yoga using the shamanic structure of Upper, Middle and Lower World as a reference point. It is, by no means, complete. However, to the best of my knowledge, no such other comparison exists.

In her 1978 book, *Kabbalah, The Way of the Jewish Mystic* (Shambala Publications Inc.), Perle Epstein spends three and one-half pages on "Parallels To Taoist Meditation" at the end of a chapter on Jewish Kabbalistic practices (pp. 69-72). Her information was scant, but it is the only reference I've ever previously seen to any similarity between the Jewish Kabbalists and Taoist Yoga. There may be others. This is not a scholarly, exhaustive work.

Western Kabbalists often wrote about the Taoists. They have adopted the *I Ching* which, according to legend, was created by the Taoist sage Fu Shih over 5,000 years ago, as a system of divination. Now it appears that the Microcosmic Orbit and sexual practices are also making the crossover. For too long, the practices of both the Western Kabbalists and the Taoists were secret, so there was actually little available to compare. As I have stated before, as time goes on the exchange of information and practice will continue between the two groups. I hope this book lays the groundwork for future exploration.

There seems to me to be little chance that Jewish Kabbalists will be able to adopt much of the Western Kabbalists or the Taoists into their system. But, there is nothing wrong with this. Jewish Kabbalism is truly a religious system in every sense of the word, while both Western Kabbalism and Taoist Yoga are not. They can be considered a way of life, or a personal philosophy but, strictly speaking, they are not a religion. Taoism is a religion that is now almost extinct. It is not synonymous with Taoist Yoga. There is absolutely no need to be a Taoist to practice Taoist Yoga. Mantak Chia is a Christian, for example. A Western Kabbalist can belong to any religion. A Jewish Kabbalist, by definition, must be Jewish.

Jewish Kabbalism is enjoying a resurgence. Meditation has again become a fashionable practice for the Hebrew mystics. I hope that my chapter on the *Sepher Yetzirah* will add some new food for thought. My research for this chapter was original. It probably deserves an entire book to fully elucidate these new directions. Only Divine Providence knows what the future holds.

Taoist Yoga will continue to expand, slowly, throughout the world. The first-time availability of its practices and the undeniable benefits of the system make this a certainty. As I write, Mantak Chia has moved back to his native Thailand. He opened the door for many to follow.

It occurs to me that I may not have clearly defined the ultimate goals of Kabbalism and Taoist Yoga for they were the same. The goal was immortality. For the Taoist, the method is to grow and mature the immortal spirit body and eventually become an immortal sage. For the Kabbalist, both Jewish and Western, the goal is the same. The method was to find and eat the fruit of the Tree of Life. As a concept (not a diagram), the Tree of Life first appears in Chapter 2 of Genesis and again in Chapter 3. In Chapter 3, the serpent tempts Eve and she and then Adam eat the fruit of the Tree of the Knowledge of Good and Evil and they are expelled from Eden. As the story is popularly understood, it was the eating of the fruit of the Tree of the Knowledge of Good and Evil that was the reason for the expulsion. But, this is not so. I'll let the Bible speak for itself: (Gen. 3:22–24)

> 22. And the Lord God said, Behold the man is become as one of us, to know good and evil, and now, lest he put forth his hand and take also of the Tree of Life, and eat, and live forever.
>
> 23. Therefore, the Lord God sent him forth from the Garden of Eden, to till the ground from whence he was taken.
>
> 24. So he drove out the man, and he placed at the east of the Garden the Cherubim, and the flaming sword which turned everyway, to keep the path to the Tree of Life."

So, we see the real reason for the expulsion: to keep man from reaching the Tree of Life and gaining immortality. Somewhere in each of us is an Adam or Eve in exile, seeking the way back to the Garden of Eden. The goal is to gain entrance and eat from the Tree of Life (or if you are a Taoist to find the Golden Flower). The way was guarded by the Cherubim. My final piece of information then, is that the Cherubim are the Angels of Yesod in the world of Assiah. Use this information wisely. It's a new age that we live in.

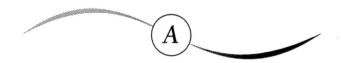

# Appendix

## Meditations

All of the meditations on the following pages, except the Healing Love meditation which was given by Mantak Chia, are transcribed, with a little editing, from classes I have held over the years.

The meditations are self-explanatory. You can refer to the appropriate text and diagrams before doing the meditation. There is no set time or place for them to be done. However the Fusion of the Five Elements is best when done in the morning.

The meditations work best if they are read to you or recorded on a tape recorder and listened to through headphones. There is a great deal of information contained in them. If you are reading them, you should be able to get great benefit from them as long as you're not distracted.

You don't have to do an entire meditation. You can pick out parts that you like or want to work with. The important thing is regular daily practice.

A note on Taoist meditations. Colors associated with the five major organs and five elements are used in the meditations. For the kidneys and Water Element, I use the color sapphire blue. This is how I learned it. The traditional Taoist color for the water Element is black. Feel free to substitute black for sapphire blue if it feels more comfortable to you.

So, here they are, have fun with them.

## *Taoist Meditation 1*

### THE INNER SMILE AND THE SIX HEALING SOUNDS

Sit up straight in your chair, without using the back of the chair to support you.

Keep your knees fairly close together, and both feet on the ground.

Place your left hand in your lap, palm facing upward. Clasp this hand with the right hand, palm facing downward. Allow the clasped hands to rest in your lap.

Close your eyes and sit quietly for a moment.

Place your point of concentration on the tip of your nose—as if looking down at the tip of the nose. Try and get in touch with the feeling at the tip of the nose. It may tingle. Can you concentrate on the tip or does it seem that there is a pull to the left or to the right? Try and establish a balance so that it feels as if the right eye is looking down at the right tip and the left eye is looking down at the left tip, with no pulling in either direction. Sit like this for a few moments.

Breathe easily and relax.

Now slowly bring your point of concentration up to a point just above the bridge of the nose, to the point between and just above the two eyes. Not quite as high as the eyebrows but above the bridge of the nose. This point is known as the Mid-Eyebrow or Third Eye.

Now imagine that just in front of you, at a distance you feel comfortable with, is someone you love or admire very dearly. This person is smiling at you. They are smiling right into your eyes. Your eyes light up with a smile and you smile back at them.

Feel the smile move into your left eye. And then into the right eye. Feel as if both eyes are actually smiling. The two eyes are the positive poles in the body. It is in the eyes that the work of restoring positive energy begins. Feel the smile in the outer corner of the left eye. Feel it at the bottom of the left eye, then the top of the left eye. Feel the inner corner of the left eye smile. Feel the inside of the eye smile. Then the back of the left eye. Feel the whole left eye smiling, the whole eyeball and the socket.

Now, we do the same for the right eyeball. Feel the outer corner smile ... the bottom ... the top ... the inner corner ... the interior of the right eye ... and the back of the eye. Feel the eye relax with smiling, loving energy.

Feel as if both eyes are smiling. Now, lift up the outer corners of your lips into a smile. Feel your cheekbones raise up and the outer corners of your eyes crinkle up into a real smile. Now, your whole face is smiling.

Now reestablish your connection with the smiling face of your loved one. If you like, you can see this face transform into a smiling, golden sun. Feel the smiling golden energy enter into your eyes and feel your eyes smiling. Continue to lift up the corners of your mouth toward the outer corners of your eyes. Now, feel a real smile. When you can really smile like this, you feel good, you feel relaxed. When you're really smiling like this, it's impossible to feel sad or depressed. The more you smile, the more habitual it becomes, so it becomes easier and easier to smile.

Now, raise the tip of your tongue to your upper palate just behind your teeth. And let it remain there. Now, feel the smiling energy move down to the roof of your mouth. Feel the roof of your mouth relax and smile. This area is often very tense without our even realizing it. It is as if our eyesight were reversed and we are looking downward into ourself.

Move the smile down into the center of the chest, behind the breastbone. As you do this, your neck relaxes and contracts like a turtle's neck withdrawing into the body.

The eyes continue to smile into the center of the chest. This is the area of the thymus gland. To the Taoists, the thymus gland is the organ of rejuvenation. As we age, it gets smaller and seems to shrivel up. So, smile into the thymus gland and feel it begin to grow and blossom, like a flower opening up. Stay here as long as you like.

Next, move the smile into the left side of the chest, into the heart. Smile into your heart. Say hello to your heart. Thank it for beating and keeping your blood circulating. Feel your heart. You might feel it loosen up and relax. Feel it open and blossom like a flower.

Now, we are going to do the healing sound for the heart. H-a-a-w-w. Inhale and slowly vocalize the sound as you exhale. Smile down and do the healing sound as if it were coming right from the center of your heart. Inhale. Exhale and make the sound H-a-a-w-w. Feel any negativity in the heart. Feel any impatience, feel any hatred melt away like gray smoke and pass right out of your body. So, inhale one more time and exhale. H-a-a-w-w.

Now, quietly keep your concentration on your heart and visualize your heart surrounded by brilliant red light. Feel your heart bask in the red light and fill with the positive emotions of love and joy. Do the healing sound one more time. H-a-a-w-w. And feel your heart smiling with joy and love.

Next, we smile into our lungs. As you inhale through your nose, feel a connection between the nostrils and the lungs. Smile to the lungs, thank them for breathing and keeping you alive. Feel the lungs relax and expand. The healing sound for the lungs is s-s-s-s-s. Inhale and then exhale while slowly making the healing sound s-s-s-s-s. The negative emotions associated by the Taoists with the lungs is sadness and depression. As we make the healing sound and smile into the lungs, imagine that any feeling of sadness or depression just break up and like gray smoke just pass right out of the body. Do the healing sound again. Inhale, then exhale s-s-s-s-s. Smile down into the lungs. Feel sadness and depression leave.

Now, imagine that the lungs are surrounded by a metallic white light. Like a metallic white metal, cool and crisp. And as you again do the healing sound s-s-s-s-s, you feel the positive emotions of courage and righteousness fill the lungs. Sit up straight in your seat and feel confident and courageous.

Now, reestablish the smile in your eyes. Lift up the corners of your mouth, crinkle up the outer corners of your eyelids. Feel that smiling sun and one more time see the white metallic light surround and full the lungs. Do the healing sound one more time. Inhale. Exhale s-s-s-s-s. Sound it directly in the lungs.

Now, we are going to move the smiling energy into the liver. The liver is a large organ on the right side of the body behind the lower part of the rib cage, beneath the lungs. Smile down to the liver. See if you can feel something there on the right side. Say hello to the liver. Thank it for aiding in digestion and detoxifying the body. The healing sound of the liver is sh-h-h-h.

So inhale and then exhale and slowly do the sound. Do you feel any heat coming out of the liver? Can you feel it relax? Now, smile down to the liver. The negative emotion associated with the liver is anger. Smile down and make the healing sound sh-h-h-h. Feel the anger and the heat melt out of the liver like gray smoke and pass out of your body. Sh-h-h-h.

Sit up in your chair, smile down to the liver and visualize the liver surrounded by a brilliant emerald green light. The Taoists referred to the liver as the Green Dragon. So, visualize the liver filled and surrounded by the color of the Green Dragon. Feel the liver begin to fill with its positive emotion—kindness.

Think of some kindness that you've done for some person, maybe a stranger with no thought of reward or some kindness someone did for you that they didn't have to do and how good it made you feel and how it made you smile. And sense how the positive emotions and the smile and the sound tie together. Now, one more time reestablish the smile. Lift the corners of the lips and crinkle the corners of the eyes and smile down into the liver, see it surrounded by bright emerald light and do the healing sound sh-h-h-h right inside the liver. Sense that kindness. Can you feel the liver now? Is it tingling, or bubbling, or softening up?

If you feel like rocking in your seat, that is O.K. It helps the energy move within the body. Make sure both feet are on the ground. You want to keep in touch with the earth energy.

Now, we put our concentration on our two kidneys. They are located on the back side of our body at the bottom of the rib cage. One on the left side and one on the right. The bottom of the kidneys is at a point opposite the level of the navel. Smile down to your kidneys. Thank them for filtering your blood and removing liquid waste, keeping you healthy and alive.

The healing sound for the kidneys is ch-u-w-a-a-a-y, like the word "chew" sounded quickly and "way" sounded slowly. Softly make the healing sound. Inhale. Exhale ch-u-w-a-a-a-y. Smile down to the kidneys and feel them relax and cool down.

Make the healing sound again. Inhale. Exhale as you make the sound ch-u-w-a-a-a-y. The negative emotion of the kidney is fear. When you feel afraid, the negative energy of the kidneys is controlling you. The healing sound breaks up that fear. Now, smile into the two kidneys and see them surrounded by a deep blue color—sapphire blue. All negativity melts away like gray smoke, passing right out of the body. It is replaced with the positive emotion of the kidney, gentleness. Make the healing sound again. Inhale. Exhale and make the sound ch-u-w-a-a-a-y. Feel the fear change into a sense of gentleness. As if you could sense the gentle side of nature. Smile down into the kidneys. Feel the gentleness spread out into your whole body along with the kindness, courage and joy from the other organs.

Now, move your point of concentration to the pancreas and spleen. The pancreas runs across the body at waist level from the bottom of the liver across to the left side where it is intimately connected with the spleen which is a fist-sized organ on the left side of the body at the bottom of the front rib cage.

Smile into the pancreas. Thank it for producing insulin and regulating your blood sugar level. And smile into the spleen and thank it for silently doing its work of producing antibodies to fight off disease.

The healing sound for the spleen and pancreas is wh-o-o-o-o, like the word "who" sounded out slowly. You might actually feel the sound vibrate more in the area of the solar plexus when it is sounded out upon exhalation. So smile down to the spleen. Smile down to the pancreas. Make the healing sound wh-o-o-o-o. Can you sense a tightness in the solar plexus area?

The negative emotion of the spleen-pancreas is worry. So, smile down to the spleen-pancreas and make the healing sound again.

Inhale. Exhale, make the sound wh-o-o-o-o and feel worry become like a dark gray smoke and dissipate from your body. Imagine your spleen, your pancreas, the whole midsection going to the left side of the body, surrounded by a brilliant yellow color. Smile down into the bright yellow color and feel as if you're expanding. Feel openness. Feel open to all the things you are learning in this meditation. Feel that you're open to other people. That you're calm enough to listen to other people, to hear what they say. That you can listen with fairness.

Make the healing sound wh-o-o-o-o and see the bright yellow color smile down to the spleen.

One more time, make the healing sound wh-o-o-o-o and smile down to the spleen. Feel yourself open up.

We've now smiled into the five major organs. Now, smile down to your genital area. See the whole area bathed in a pink color. Smile and feel the whole genital region grow cooler and more relaxed. Smile into the genital region and thank it for performing the functions of producing life, removing waste and providing pleasure. Smile and feel love, joy, kindness, gentleness, friendliness and courage flow into the genital organs. This helps you to get in touch with your sexual desires and begin to bring them under control. You should control your sexual energy, not be controlled by it. Now, return your smile to your eyes.

## THE MIDDLE LINE

Reestablish the smile in your eyes.

What I want you to do now is to swallow saliva in the Taoist manner. We want to increase the flow of saliva in the mouth. The way to do this is to put the tip of your tongue between the front of your teeth and the back of your lips. Circle the tongue around nine times in either direction. Circle all the way around.

When you have done this, put the tip of the tongue behind the teeth and circle six times in the opposite direction than before. Feel the mouth fill with saliva. Now, smile into the saliva. It will act like a magnet to hold the smiling energy. Imagine a smiling sun radiating happiness and absorb it into the saliva.

Place the tip of your tongue on the roof of your mouth, pull your chin in and tighten the neck muscles and with a gulping sound swallow the saliva, forcing it down.

Feel the inner smile travel down your throat and esophagus and into the stomach. Feel it continue to move through all the organs of digestion. Smile into the small intestines which are about seven yards long in the middle of the abdomen.

Smile into the large intestines, the ascending colon, starting on the right side by the hip bone, then across the transverse colon to the left side and down the descending colon, into the sigmoid colon which lies within the pelvis and finally into the rectum and anus. The large intestines are about a yard and a half long.

Now reestablish the smile in your eyes and see if you can feel that smiling sensation throughout your entire digestive system. Lift up the corners of your mouth and crinkle the outer corners of the eyes.

## THE BACK LINE

Feel the smiling energy move into the left side of your brain. Inside just the left side of the brain. Forget about everything else. Feel the whole left side just light up and smile and relax. Feel the whole left side of the brain isolated. Feel the smile move back and forth, up and down and all around the left side of the brain.

Now, move the smile over to the right side of the brain and forget about everything else except that smiling right side of the brain. Feel it light up. Move the smile around upwards, backwards, down, and around and feel the whole right side of the brain smiling.

Now, right between the left and right side, the wall between the two hemispheres of the brain, feel that smiling energy go right down the center. Feel as if there is no longer any wall there. Go all the way down to the back of the head to the cerebrum and the medulla. Feel that smiling energy going back down the back of the head until it finally enters the point where the back of the skull and the neck meet.

Feel the smiling energy enter the spinal column. Now, smile into each vertebra of the seven cervical vertebra of the neck, one by one, moving slowly downward until it gets to the base of the neck and enters the spinal column itself. Feel the smiling, loving energy enter the top of the twelve thoracic (chest) vertebra and move slowly downward, one by one. Feel it descend down the back, down to the level of the heart. Then down to the level behind the solar plexus. Down to the point behind the navel where it enters the five lumbar (lower back) vertebra. Feel it continue all the way down until it reaches the triangular bone known as the sacrum. It continues to go down right through the fused vertebra of the sacrum all the way down to the coccyx, the tailbone.

Now, feel as if your whole brain and spine are filled with the smiling, loving energy. With golden light. Just relax and feel it. Now, feel the smile move up and down the spine and it spreads out into the entire nervous system. Feel all the nerves in the body, and in the arms and legs, hands and feet, fingers and toes. Feel as if your entire nervous system is smiling.

Now, move the smile back into the two eyes and we'll do the last of the six healing sounds, the Triple Warmer. As you do this, you feel like a wave is moving from the top of the head, down through your neck, through the chest, torso, abdomen, down the legs. All the way down to your feet and feel any remaining negativity in your body move right out through your fingertips and toes.

Ready. Smile in the eyes. The healing sound of the Triple Warmer is he-e-e-e-e. Feel it like a wave moving down through the body. Inhale and then exhale slowly making the healing sound. Establish the smile again. Inhale, now exhale he-e-e-e-e. Do it one more time.

Now, relax. Smile in your eyes. And we will collect energy at the navel. Put your concentration in the area just behind the navel, which is your center of balance. You want to collect the energy because we don't want to leave it scattered all through your body.

So, imagine you're forming a three-inch circle around the navel and we will move the energy from above the navel down the left side to below the navel and up on the right side. Do this nine times. Imagine energy circling around the navel nine times.

Now, reverse the direction of the circle six times and with each circle imagine the energy coming closer and closer to the center of the navel as if you're tying off a knot. And you collect the energy.

Now just relax for a minute.

Slowly open your eyes.

Rub your hands together until they get warm and massage your face, your forehead, nose, ears. This is a facial chi massage.

# *Taoist Meditation 2*

### THE MICROCOSMIC ORBIT

There are many ways to teach the Microcosmic Orbit. Different breathing techniques can be used. It can be done standing or sitting. The common denominator of all methods is to open the Governor and Functional Channels which comprise the Microcosmic Orbit.

The basic type of breathing used to help get the energy to circulate through the Orbit is called Abdominal Breathing. In this type of breathing, the lower abdomen is expanded during the inhalation of breath and contracted with the exhalation. I like to analogize it to a beach ball in the lower belly. It expands on inhalation and contracts on exhalation.

There are many variations of Abdominal Breathing. When combined with the Microcosmic Orbit, each breathing method could be used as the basis of a meditation. When done rapidly, Abdominal Breathing is known as Bellows Breathing or Quick Fire. When done slowly, it is referred to as Slow Fire.

The effectiveness of Abdominal Breathing is enhanced by pulling up on the perineum. The perineum is the point between the back of the genitals and the front of the anus. In different variations, pulling up on the perineum can be done on the inhalation, Americans seem to favor pulling up on the exhalation, and in advanced techniques the pull is maintained during the inhalation and exhalation. In the meditation here, most of the pulling up will be done during inhalation.

Sit up in your chair without using the back of the chair to support you.

Sit with your knees close together. Both feet firmly on the ground. Your hands are clasped in your lap, your left palm facing up, right palm down.

Close your eyes. Breathe regularly. Inhale. Exhale. Relax.

Put your point of concentration on the tip of your nose. Be aware of any muscular pull to the left or the right. Balance out the pull so that there is no pull to either side.

After a few moments, raise your point of concentration to the mid-eyebrow.

Imagine a friendly smiling face. It could be a loved one or a fantasy lover or it could be the smiling face of a baby. Feel the smile go directly into your eyes. Your left eye begins to smile and your right eye begins to smile. You lift up the corners of your mouth and feel your cheekbones raise and the corners of your eyes crinkle up into a smile.

The smile moves over your whole face and scalp. It moves down through your face to the roof of your mouth which relaxes as you smile. You raise the tip of your tongue to the upper palate just behind the teeth. The happy smiling energy goes down your tongue, through your throat and moves to the thymus gland in the center of your chest behind the sternum or breastbone.

Smile into your thymus gland. Feel it expand and open up and blossom like a flower. The thymus is the gland of rejuvenation. It is activated by smiling.

Smile into your heart. Surround the heart with a bright red light and feel it smile and blossom like a flower. Feel happiness in your heart.

Smile into your lungs. Surround your lungs with a metallic white color and feel your lungs smile.

Smile into your liver. Surround the liver with an emerald green light and feel your liver smiling.

Smile into your kidneys. Surround your two kidneys with a sapphire blue light and feel your kidneys smiling.

Smile into your spleen and pancreas. Surround your spleen and pancreas with a bright yellow light. Feel your spleen and pancreas smiling.

Reestablish the smile in your mid-eyebrows. Smile down to the Navel Center, the *Tan Tien*. It is right underneath the navel. Two to three inches inside. The navel is the point where we originally drew energy from our mother. It is the source of original energy. It is our Earth Center, the *Tan Tien*.

Smile into the navel. When the Navel Point is open, you feel balanced. When the navel point is closed down or obstructed it results in sloppy, picky, or distracted behavior.

Bring your concentration back to the mid-eyebrow. Be aware of the smiling energy in front of you. Inhale. Draw the energy into your mid-eyebrow. Inhale, draw energy to the thymus gland. Inhale down to the navel area.

Use the abdominal breath. Each inhalation is a small sip of air. Don't exhale unless I tell you to. Don't expand the chest as you inhale; expand your lower abdominal.

Hold your breath in your navel and feel it expand and get warmer. Exhale.

Now, inhale and exhale rapidly. Expand and contract the abdomen with short quick abdominal breaths. Breathe in and out through the nose. Do eighteen breaths. The navel area should become much warmer. This is Bellows Breathing.

Now, smile down to the Sexual Palace. For women, it is known as the Ovarian Palace and is about three inches below the navel. In men, it is known as the Sperm Palace and is located at the base of the penis beneath the pubic bone.

When the Sexual Palace is open, you have a sense of creative and personal power. When it is closed down, it is difficult to enjoy life.

Put your concentration on the Sexual Palace. Now, move the energy back and forth from the Sexual Palace back up to the Navel Point and then down again. Do it a few times as if you were washing the channel. Up then down. Inhale up to the Navel Point, exhale down to the Sexual Palace.

Smile down to the Perineum, the Gate of Life and Death. Energy can escape from this point so it must be sealed. When the perineum is open you feel grounded. When it is closed down you feel insecure.

Next you must pull the energy around the coccyx so it can rise up the spine and enter the Governor Channel. To do this you use the three step contraction method. First inhale and contract the perineum, the point between the sexual organ and the anus. Take a second sip of air and contract the anus itself. Now take a third sip of air and contract the muscle about an inch above the anus just below the coccyx. Exhale. As your technique improves, the movement becomes rhythmic.

Do the three step contraction method again. Inhale, contract the perineum, inhale again without exhaling and contract the anus. Now inhale again and contract the muscle about an inch above the anus on the backside. Feel the energy come around the lower part of the body.

Now press down on the ground with your feet and feel the energy rise up the lower part of the spine to the Sacral Point. This point is located an inch or two up from the tip of the coccyx. When the Sacral Point is open you feel balanced. When it is closed you feel as if you are imprisoned by your past.

Inhale and pull up on the perineum. The energy rises up to the Kidney Point. This is located on the spine opposite the navel. When the Kidney Point is open one feels gentleness. When it is closed you feel fear of being taken advantage of.

Move the energy down to the Sacral Point then back up to the Kidney Point. Exhale. It moves down to the Sacral Point. Inhale. It moves up to the Kidney Point. Wash the channel.

Now, inhale again, pull up on the perineum and the energy moves up the spine to the Adrenal Point. This is located opposite the solar plexus. When the Adrenal Point is open one feels a sensation of freedom. When it is closed, there is a feeling of burden and obstruction.

Again, move the energy down to the point below, the Kidney Point. Exhale down to the Kidney Point, inhale up to the Adrenal Point. Do it a few times. Wash the route, feel the channel opening.

Now, inhale again, pull up on the perineum and the energy rises up the back all the way to the base of the skull, the Jade Pillow, the Small Brain Point. When the Jade Pillow is open, you feel inspiration. When it is closed, you feel that life is suffocating.

Wash the channel. Moving the energy down to the Adrenal Point then back up to the Jade Pillow. Exhale down, inhale up.

Pull in the chin a little, straighten the neck. Inhale, pull up on the perineum and the energy rises to the Crown Point. Locate this point by imagining a line drawn from the mid-eyebrow point over the top of the head. This line intersects a second line drawn from the top of the right ear over the top of the head to the top of the left ear. The point of intersection is the Crown

Point. Three inches below the Crown Point is the Pineal Gland Point. When the Pineal Gland Point is open you can receive guidance from higher forces and you radiate happiness. When closed, you can have delusions, illusions, headaches, erratic mood swings and may feel you are a victim or slave.

Move the energy down to the Jade Pillow then back up to the Pineal Gland Point. Do this a few times. Exhale down, inhale up. Wash the channel.

Inhale again, pull up on the perineum, the energy moves down to the mid-eyebrow point. Three inches inside the skull at the mid-eyebrow point is the Pituitary Point. When the Pituitary Point is open you feel wisdom. When it is closed, there is a sense of indecision.

Move the energy back and forth between the Pineal and Pituitary Points. These points are within the brain. Feel this center of your brain expand and light up. This entire area is known as the Crystal Palace.

Make sure your tongue is raised to the upper palate directly behind the teeth. This is known as the Palate Wind Point. Further back on the hard palate is the Fire Point. Even further back at the beginning of the soft palate is the Water Point, directly beneath the pituitary gland.

Now inhale, pull up on the perineum, draw the energy all the way up to the Crown-Pineal Point. Then exhale down to the Pituitary Point, then down to the Palate Point also known as the Heavenly Pool.

By moving the tongue back and forth on the palate, the best position can be found for the energy to pass through the palate to the top of the tongue. This is experienced as a current, a sensation of electricity, coolness, warmth, tingling, numbness, or something sufficiently different to warrant attention.

Now move the energy up to the Pituitary Point and down to the Palate Point. Inhale up, exhale down. Do this a few times. Wash the channel.

Now inhale, pull up on the perineum, pull the energy up to the Crown Point. Exhale, the energy goes down through the Pituitary Point, the Palate Point, down the tongue to the Throat Point. This point is located in the lower part of the throat. It is the communication and dream center. This is traditionally a weak point that is hard to protect. When the Throat Point is open you speak more eloquently. When it is closed you feel an unwillingness to change.

Move the energy up to the Palate Point and down to the Throat Point. Do this a few times. Feel the energy going up and down the throat and tongue.

Now inhale. Pull up on the perineum, the energy rises up the spine to the Crown Point. Exhale, it descends down the Functional Channel through the Throat Point and down to the Heart Point. This point is between the nipples for men or one inch up from the bottom of the sternum (breastbone) for women. It controls the thymus gland. When the Heart Point is open love, joy, happiness, honesty and respect are felt. When it is closed one feels under attack and sorry for oneself.

Move the energy up to the Throat Point, then down to the Heart Point. Wash the channel a few times.

Exhale and the energy moves down to the Solar Plexus Point. When the Solar Plexus Point is open you feel you can take risks. When it is closed there is a sense of panic and worry.

Now move the energy up to the Heart Point and down to the Solar Plexus Point a few times. Inhale up, exhale down.

Now exhale and lower the energy to the Navel Point. Then raise the energy to the Solar Plexus Point and lower it to the Navel Point a few times. Wash the channel.

You have now completed one circulation of the Microcosmic Orbit.

Once you feel the flow of energy, it is not necessary to wash the channel. Just move the energy in a continuous orbit, using the mind to direct the *Chi*.

With the concentration on the Navel Point do a few rapid Abdominal Breaths to heat up the Navel Center. Exhale, pull up slightly on the perineum and the energy descends to the Sexual Palace. Exhale again and it goes down to the Perineum Point.

Pull up lightly on the anus and then an inch above the anus and the energy moves from the bottom of the Functional Channel into the Governor Channel to the Sacral Point.

Now inhale and the energy rises to the Kidney Point, to the Adrenal Point to the Small Brain Point (Jade Pillow) and up to the Crown Point.

Exhale and the energy descends to the Pituitary Point (or mid-eyebrows) to the Palate Point, down to the Throat Point, Heart Point, Solar Plexus Point and back to the Navel Point.

Do as many circulations as you want to.

At the end of the meditation, you collect the energy at the navel. Circle energy clockwise around the navel either nine or thirty-six times. This circle is about three inches wide. Starting an inch and one-half above the navel, circle from above to the left side of the navel, to below the navel. Come up on the right side.

Now reverse the direction. Do this six or twenty-four times. The energy moves counter-clockwise. As you come to the final circulations around the navel, pull the energy closer and closer to the navel and then directly into the navel on the final circle.

May the *Chi* be with you.

# *Taoist Meditation 3*

### FUSION OF THE FIVE ELEMENTS

Sit up straight in your seat, not using the back of the chair to support you.

Place your left hand in your lap, palm up. Cover with your right hand, palm down, so that your hands are clasped in your lap.

Put your concentration on the tip of your nose. Feel a tingling at the tip of the nose. Be aware if there is a pull of the muscles more to the left or to the right. Try and balance it out. The Taoists found that doing this, looking down toward the tip of the nose, was the fastest way to gather the energy together and concentrate the mind.

Now move the point of concentration up to the point between and slightly above the two eyes. This is the Third Eye, or Mid-Eyebrow Point.

Imagine that a few feet in front of you can feel the warmth of the sun. Picture a happy smiling face on the sun, smiling into your eyes. Feel your eyes smile back. Lift up the outer corners of the mouth, raise them toward the eyes. Feel your cheeks lift up and the outer corners of your eyes crinkle up a little bit as you smile. Feel a real smile in your eyes. Imagine your left eye is smiling and your right eye is smiling.

Raise the tip of your tongue to the roof of your mouth. And looking inward as if you could turn your eyes and see inside yourself, smile to the roof of your mouth. Feel the roof of your mouth soften. It seems to rise up and expand.

Now, smile down through your tongue and into your heart and feel that smiling, loving energy in your heart.

Feel it expand into the lungs.

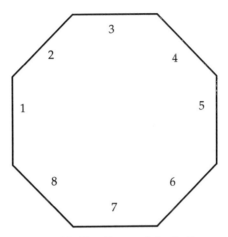

Figure 32: First Layer of the *Pa Qua*

Then into the liver.

Smile into the kidneys.

Now, smile into the spleen.

Now, reestablish that smile in your eyes. And we're going to swallow saliva down our throat. To do that we put our tongue between the teeth and the outer lips and circle the tongue nine times.

Then, reverse, putting the tongue behind the teeth and circling in the other direction six times.

Now imagine that you're chewing the saliva, moving the jaw back and forth. And while you're doing this fill the saliva with the happy smiling golden energy from the smiling sun. Now raise your tongue to the roof of your mouth, pull in the chin, straighten your neck and with a gulping sound swallow that saliva. Feel it move down through the esophagus and into the stomach, through the small intestine, feeling it moving

**Figure 33: The Complete *Pa Qua***

quickly through the large intestines to the colon. Through the entire digestive tract from the throat to the anus, feel that smiling, loving energy.

Reestablish that smile in your eyes. Feel that smile center now in the point between the two eyes. Feel your neck growing heavy. Your head growing heavy. And like a turtle pulling its head into its shell, feel your head sink down. Your neck grows loose. All the tension and tightness in the neck melts away.

Smile now from the eyes into the left side of the brain.

Then smile into the right side of the brain.

Feel the smile go right down the center of the brain, between the two hemispheres, down past the cerebrum and the medulla, into the neck and the smile passes through each vertebra in the neck. Feel the smile quickly moving down and enter the spine itself and quickly move down from the level of the top of the shoulders to the point behind the heart, down to the point behind the solar plexus, down to the point behind the navel, down through the vertebra of the sacrum and all the way down to the coccyx.

Now smile into your sexual organs.

Now bring your concentration back up to the point between your two eyes. We're now going to begin building the *Pa Qua* in the front of the body. The *Pa Qua* is built up of eight sides. It is formed inside the body, behind the navel, about three inches wide.

You can begin on the left side. A line straight up at the left side of the navel. Then connect that line with a 45-degree line to the top. At the top a straight line across. Then a line 45 degrees downward on the right. Then a line straight down. Another line 45 degrees down to the bottom. A line across the bottom. Then the eighth line is 45 degrees upwards.

We've created the first layer of the web. Now inside that layer form a second layer. Then inside of that, form a third layer.

At each intersection of the angles of the layer, draw a straight line inward so that there are eight lines inward, cutting the *Pa Qua* into eight sections and in the center visualize the *Tai Chi* symbol.

This is an energy net. A Taoist energy collector. We're going to use this *Pa Qua* to collect the element energy from the organs.

The organ we'll begin with is the kidneys. Using your mind, concentrate and look inward towards the back, the bottom of the rib cage on the back on the left and right side. Feel the two kidneys. Try to sense the two kidney organs, on the backside above the level of the navel.

Now, take a deep breath pushing down on the diaphragm. Without exhaling, pull in on the abdomen and take another breath. Now, take a third breath and pull up on the perineum. And at the level of the perineum, visualize a ball of energy. Exhale and we'll do it again. Inhale, pushing the diaphragm down. Take another sip of air, pull in the abdomen. Take a third sip, pull up the perineum. Now as you pull up, sense a connection on the left side between the kidney and the perineum. Now pull up and sense a connection on the right side between the kidney and the perineum.

Exhale.

You may want to move around or rock your body as you sit.

Inhale again, pulling up on the perineum and sense a ball there. A collection point about three inches wide. Draw the energy down from the kidneys. Feel the energy from the kidneys moving down to the collection point at the perineum.

The energy from the kidneys is cold. Its color is deep sapphire blue. So sense that cold blue energy collecting at the perineum. You might actually sense real cold energy and, if you can't actually feel it, just imagine it; the coldness drawing into the perineum.

Now, we put our concentration on our heart. Move your point of concentration to the heart and feel the heat there.

Form a collection point in the center of the chest, beneath the breastbone, approximately three inches wide. Feel a flow of heat from the heart into that collection point. It's as if you could move inside that collection point yourself, or move your mind into it and will the hot energy to gather into the collection point. The mind moves the energy, and the energy or chi follows. So use your mind to draw the chi from your heart into the heart collection point in the center of the chest.

See the red color. You can even imagine a small flame burning
in the center of your chest. See that flame burning with the
bright red color of the Fire energy from the heart. Feel the heat.

Now, you're going to split your concentration in two. Part of
your concentration goes down to the perineum collection
point. The other part of your concentration remains at the collection point in the center of your chest. Exhale and as you
inhale pull up on the perineum and feel that cold energy drawn
up your body into the *Pa Qua* behind your navel. Exhale and
feel the hot energy move down to the *Pa Qua* as you relax the
perineum. Inhale and pulling up on the perineum feel the cold
chi rise to the *Pa Qua*. Exhale and feel the hot energy descend.
Continue doing this. Inhale and pull the cold energy up, then
exhale, relax the perineum, and pull the hot energy down.
Keep it in the center of your body in the *Pa Qua* which acts like
a web to collect and hold the hot and cold energies.

You feel, in the middle of your body, this cold energy and this
hot energy mixing together. Start consciously mixing the hot
and cold *chi* inside the *Tai Chi* symbol in the center of the *Pa
Qua*. The web pulls it in and holds the chi. It can't escape from
the web. The web draws the cold towards the center and draws
the heat towards the center and it mixes and blends there.

Now put your concentration on the right side of your body, on
the liver. The liver is a large organ on the right side below the
lung, under the rib cage. Feel it there. The energy of the liver is
warm and damp or moist. See if you can sense that warm, damp
*chi*. You might feel the palms of your hands begin to sweat.

The collection point for the liver is on the line straight down
from the nipple at the right side of the navel. Feel a round
collection point form there. Feel it begin to draw this warm,
damp energy down. Feel it moving right out of the liver down

to the collection point. The color of the liver energy is emerald green. Bright green. See and feel that green-colored chi filling the collection point on the right side of the *Pa Qua* at the navel, this glowing emerald green ball. This is wood energy, the chi of the liver. Leave this ball at the right side of the *Pa Qua*.

Now, put your concentration on your lungs. The left lung and the right lung. The chi of the lungs is cool and dry. Like a piece of metal, cool and dry to the touch. Not as cold as the water energy. Cool and dry.

The collection point for the lung energy is on the left side of the body, opposite the liver collection point. So on a point straight down from the left nipple, just outside the *Pa Qua* at the navel, form a three-inch ball. Feel this cool, dry energy being drawn from both lungs. It may feel as if energy from the right lung is being drawn into the left lung and then being pulled straight down. Or it may feel as if the chi is coming simultaneously from the left and right lungs directly into the collection point.

The color of the lung energy is metallic white and its element is metal. See that metallic white color fill the collection point, drawing the chi from the lungs to the collection point on the left side of the *Pa Qua*.

Now again we split our concentration to the liver collection point on the right side and the lung collection point on the left side. We spiral the energy from both into the *Pa Qua*. Feel the wood and metal energies spiraling in, joining with the fire energy of the heart and the water energy of the kidneys. The ancient Taoists referred to the wood chi as the Green Dragon and to the metal chi as the White Tiger. So we mix the Green Dragon and the White Tiger with the fire energy of the heart, which is Heavenly Energy, and the water energy of the kidneys, which is an Earthly Energy. We mix the four energies or elements in the *Pa Qua* in the center of the body.

Now, put your concentration on the spleen on the left side of the body. Sense a fist-sized organ at the lower left part of the rib cage. The energy of the spleen is neutral. It's not hot, it's not cold. It's not cool or dry or warm or moist. Neutral energy. We spiral the chi of the spleen directly into the *Pa Qua*. Its color is bright yellow. See this yellow energy spiraling right into the *Pa Qua* mixing with the other four energies. The element of the spleen chi is earth. So mix the earth chi with the other four elements: Fire, water, wood, and metal.

Now, put your concentration right into the center of the Pa Qua, into the Tai Chi symbol, and feel all the elements blend together. Feel the hot fire energy, the cold energy of the water, the warm damp energy of the wood, the cool dry energy of the metal mixing with the neutral energy of the earth in the center of your body.

Now, on your back, directly opposite your front *Pa Qua*, picture a second *Pa Qua*. Just duplicate it, as if you had a mental copy machine. Now picture a collection ball at the level of your sacrum, just above the lowest point of the spine, just above the coccyx.

Feel that little ball three inches wide. Feel it collecting any of the residual cold water energy.

Now above, picture a collection point just inside the spine, opposite the heart collection point. Feel the hot energy from the heart, any residual energy, rushing to that collection point.

Now inhale, pull up on the perineum and feel the cold energy rise up to the *Pa Qua* on the back,. Exhale and feel the hot energy move down to the *Pa Qua*. Inhale, pull up and feel the cold energy rise up the spine. Exhale, feel the hot energy move down. Feel the two energies mixing in the *Pa Qua* on your back so that the *Pa Qua* is neither hot nor cold any longer.

Now, on the right side form a three-inch ball at the level of the navel. Collect the residual moist, warm energy of the liver. If it helps you to use the colors, by all means use them. The color of the wood chi is emerald green.

Now, on the left side, form a three-inch ball at the level of the navel and collect the residual cool, dry energy of the metal, the lung chi. And spiral these two energies, the wood and the metal into the back *Pa Qua*. So you've now mixed the energy of the fire and the water and the wood and the metal. On the back, we do not mix in the earth energy of the spleen. The earth energy is only mixed into the front *Pa Qua*.

Now, on the right side form a third *Pa Qua* at the same level as the other two. Quickly form a ball at the level of the hip and feel any cold water energy remaining on the right side drawn to this collection point.

And above at the level of the heart, just under the armpit, create another collection point. Collect any residual hot energy. Pull up on the perineum and inhale and feel that cold energy rise into the *Pa Qua*. Exhale and relax the perineum and the hot energy descends into the *Pa Qua*.

The web holds that energy. The *Pa Qua* web holds the energy and draws it into the *Tai Chi* symbol.

Now, behind the *Pa Qua* at your right side, on your back, form another collection point. Gather the cool, dry energy of the lungs there. And on the front side form another collection ball and draw any residual energy from the liver, the moist, warm wood chi. Spiral these two elements, the wood and the metal from the front and the back into the right side *Pa Qua*.

Now, we repeat this process on the left side. Form a *Pa Qua* on the left side.

Form a collection ball at the left hip. Draw in any remaining cold energy. Form another collection point at the level of the heart, under the left armpit. Draw in any residual hot energy.

Draw the fire and water energies into the *Pa Qua* on the left side. Inhale, pull up on the perineum, feel the cold energy rise into the *Pa Qua*. Exhale, relax the perineum, and feel the hot energy descent into the *Pa Qua*.

If you can, you can draw both elements simultaneously, using your mind to direct the *chi* from below and above.

Now, behind you, on the left side form another collection point. Draw in the energy of the metal.

And in front, form the final collection point, and draw in the wood energy from the liver.

Spiral these two into the left *Pa Qua*. Mix it with the fire and water chi. Blend all the elements together.

You have now collected the energy of all your major organs into four *Pa Quas*. One in the front. One on the back and on the right side and left side. All the *Pa Quas* are within the body, under the skin.

Now, we are going to spiral all those energies into the very center of our body. About three and one-half inches inside of us. Behind the navel. Beginning with the front *Tai Chi*.

Feel the front *Tai Chi* symbol begin to spin. Feel it begin to spin in whatever direction you feel comfortable with.

Now, feel the *Tai Chi* symbol on the back also begin to spin. It could be in the same direction as on the front *Tai Chi*, it could be in the opposite direction.

Feel them spiral toward each other. Right into the center of your body. We call this the Cauldron, the *Tan Tien*. Spiral the energy from the front *Tai Chi* and the back *Tai Chi*. The blended energy of the five elements. The fire, water, wood, metal and earth.

Blend it and harmonize it in the center of your body.

Now, from the left and right sides spiral the energy from the two *Tai Chi* symbols into the Cauldron. Spiral in from the left side. Spiral in from your right side.

If you like, you can reverse the spiral. Feel it move in different directions. See if the energy is stronger either way. You can play with the chi. Feel it.

Now, at the very center of your body feel that energy begin to grow very strong. It congeals. It congeals into a Pearl.

Spiral from the front and back, the left side and the right side. Feel the Pearl, sense it. See it if you can. A gleaming pearl. You can see it silvery white or golden. Shining. Feel it contract more and more so that it's no bigger than a pin head.

Keep drawing energy in from the front, back, right and left and the Pearl expands. Now, take that Pearl. You're going to move it.

Move the Pearl down to the perineum. Use the three step contraction method. Contract the perineum, then contract the anus, finally contract the muscle above the anus just below the coccyx. The Pearl enters the coccyx. It rises up the spine, up the backbone. Past the sacrum, past the Door of Life behind the navel, past the solar plexus and the heart, to the back of the neck, through the neck. Pull in the chin a little bit, raise your tongue to the roof of your mouth. Pull up on the perineum. Feel that Pearl go up to the top of your head.

Now, direct it downward. Exhale. Direct it down with your Third Eye. Down through the tip of your nose. Keep the tip of your tongue raised and feel the Pearl move from the tip of your nose into your tongue and down through your throat, through your esophagus, past the solar plexus and down to your navel. Collect the Pearl into the Cauldron, the *Tan Tien*.

Feel the Pearl there.

Let go of the *Pa Quas*. The *Pa Qua* in the front and the back, the left and right sides all dissolve.

We begin to collect energy into the navel. From above the navel, about an inch and one-half above, circle from above to the left of the navel to below the navel. Come up on the right side. Do this nine times. This is clockwise.

Then reverse the direction of the energy. Do it counter-clockwise six times. And draw it directly into the navel on the final circle.

Take a deep breath. Relax. Slowly return to the room.

Rub the palms of your hands together until they get warm and massage your face.

As you practice and become more proficient, you can do the Fusion much faster. Form the *Pa Quas*. Form the collection points. Draw the energy in. But, it takes practice.

# Taoist Meditation 4

### HEALING LOVE—THE GOD AND GODDESS

This meditation is adopted from the final Teacher Training session held in the United States at Vassar College on July 21, 1994 just prior to Mantak Chia's return to Thailand.

It is an advanced meditation designed to get you in touch with your sexual energy and then connect you to what I can only describe as cosmic sexual energy.

The meditation will make use of the three *Tan Tiens*: 1) Lower *Tan Tien*—behind the navel, 2) Middle *Tan Tien* has two versions—one at the solar plexus and one in the heart, and 3) Upper *Tan Tien* in the center of the brain—the Crystal Palace.

The three *Tan Tien* are interconnected and are also connected to the Microcosmic Orbit.

STEP I: THE THREE *TAN TIENS*: Begin by sitting up in your seat. You should sit far forward on the seat so that the sexual organs are past the edge. Males should wear loose-fitting underwear that allows the testicles to hang freely. Clasp hands, left hand up in palm.

Close your eyes. Imagine that you can turn your eyes all the way around inside your skull looking up, then down, then within from bottom to top. Physically, this cannot be actually done. But, by looking downward and pulling in on the eye muscles and simultaneously pulling up on the testicles or the lips of the vagina, you actually feel that the eyes are rolling backward and around.

The left eye is *yang*. This is symbolized by a young boy. The right eye is *yin* symbolized by a young girl.

Inhale. Men, look down toward the testicles. Women, look down toward your ovaries. Exhale. Men, pull up on the testicles, then the perineum, the anus and an inch below the coccyx. Women, pull the Jing from the ovaries to the lips of the vagina, gently pull the lips of the vagina closed, then the anus and an inch below the coccyx. The eyes direct *Jing* sexual energy from the testicles or from the ovaries and lips of the vagina, into the opening of the coccyx and up the spine to a point behind the lower *Tan Tien* at the navel, the Door of Life. Imagine that you are pouring the Jing sexual energy into the lower *Tan Tien* which you can visualize as a cauldron standing on three legs. Inhale and look downward. The sexual organs are relaxed. Exhale, pull up on the testicles or draw sexual energy from the ovaries to the lips of the vagina, close lips of the vagina and pull upward and backward. The *Jing* energy rises up the spine and is poured directly into the cauldron behind the navel.

As the eyes seem to turn inward, you actually feel the testicles moving.

Do this a total of nine times.

After the ninth exhalation, rolling of the eyes, and raising of the sexual energy to the lower *Tan Tien*, we begin raising the energy nine times to the Middle *Tan Tien* behind the solar plexus.

It is done in the same manner. Inhale. The eyes turn downward from above to below. Genitals are relaxed. Exhale. Pull in on the eye muscles. The eyes seem to turn inward. Pull up on the sexual organ and jing energy rises up the spine to a point slightly above the solar plexus and pours into the cauldron at the solar plexus.

Do this nine times.

Now, we will raise the *Jing* sexual energy to the Upper *Tan Tien*. You should be feeling a connection between the eyes and the sexual organs when you pull in or up on them. This process is called Turning the Water Wheel.

So, once again we inhale and look from above to below. Exhale. Pull in on the eye muscles as inner eyesight turns past the genitals. Pull up on the sexual organs and the eyes direct the jing up the spine, through the neck and up to the top of the head where it is poured down into the Upper *Tan Tien* or Cauldron.

This is done nine times.

The sexual energy that is brought up to each cauldron is allowed to remain there. However, you might feel it seem to drip down to the cauldron beneath it or all the way back down to the sexual organs. This is okay.

STEP II: THE HEART AND KIDNEY CONNECTION: IRRIGATING THE HEART: When you feel impatient or tense, your heart seems to push toward the front of your body. In Step II, we relax the heart and seem to pull it back further into our body.

To accomplish this, you do the heart healing sound, h-a-a-w-w.

This removes heat from the heart. We then pour this heat down to the kidneys and the psoas muscles in the lumbar area of the lower back.

Inhale and direct your concentration to your heart. Exhale slowly making the healing sound, h-a-a-w-w. You feel heat coming out of the heart. It seems to move back toward the spine.

Now direct it down to the kidneys. The energy of the kidneys is normally cold especially when you feel fear. The heat from the heart warms up the kidneys.

Repeat this process at least six times doing the heart healing sound and bringing the hot energy down to the two kidneys. Next, exhale down to the psoas muscle in the lumbar area of the lower back. This muscle spreads out from the spine and has a tendency to contract and cause lower back pain and stiffness. The psoas muscle does not like cold. Too much cold kidney energy causes it to contract. When you feel fear, it contracts. When the psoas muscles are warmed up, they relax.

So, exhale and allow the hot energy to overflow from the kidneys down to the psoas muscle. Do this six times. Feel the psoas muscle warm up and relax.

Allow your concentration to move down your legs and into the ground. From the earth itself, inhale and pull up cold sapphire blue water energy. This energy rises past the psoas muscles to the kidneys. From the kidneys, it rises up the spine and is poured back into the heart. This is called Irrigating the Heart.

The heart is then pulled back by doing the heart healing sound and we repeat the entire Step II process.

STEP III: MALE AND FEMALE: Picture in your heart a perfectly formed naked male.

Picture in your sexual organs a perfectly formed naked female.

(You can reverse the position of the male and female if it makes you more comfortable).

Bring the male and female to the top of your head. They are both beautiful. They are totally attracted to each other. The male is pure *yang* and the female is pure *yin*. They begin having sexual intercourse at the top of your head. Use your imagination. Take as much time as you like. Engage in foreplay if you like.

STEP IV: THE GOD AND GODDESS: Imagine above the male and female having sex that a naked male god and goddess appear. They are the most handsome and beautiful beings you have ever seen. The male god is well-muscled with a well formed erect male sexual organ. The goddess is awesomely beautiful with a perfect figure, beautiful breasts and vagina.

Suspended in space above your head they begin having sex. Feel the intensity and excitement grow. Imagine that you can feel them moving together.

They produce a sexual fluid that drips down from above as they continue copulating. This cosmic sexual fluid drips down from above into your brain. It fills your brain with feelings of ecstacy.

Allow the brain to fill with this heavenly sexual fluid, then let it flow down the front channel into your heart.

When your heart fills up, it flows down into the solar plexus.

When the solar plexus fills, the cosmic sexual fluid flows down to the navel.

When the navel area fills, the sexual fluid flows down to the genitals.

STEP V: THE POWER LOCK OR BIG DRAW: Once the heavenly sexual fluid is brought down to the genitals, you do the Big Draw to bring this energy up the spine and into the brain. Inhale a short deep breath of air. Then push the tongue up to the roof of the mouth and clench the teeth. Pull the chin inward toward the back of the neck. Pull in the muscles of the eyes and look upward and inward toward the Upper *Tan Tien*. Contract the anus and pull up on the genitals, perineum and buttocks. This activates the sacral pump which sends the sexual energy up the spine.

Clench the fists and arms. Use your toes to claw into the ground. Keep the shoulders and chest relaxed.

All of this is done at the same time and is not as complicated as it sounds.

Sexual energy is drawn up the spine and into the brain. Spiral it there.

If you're a man, draw this energy down to the navel. It is too hot to keep in the head.

If you're a woman, you can leave the sexual energy in the brain. It's much cooler than the male sexual energy.

Now, you can take a deep breath and relax.

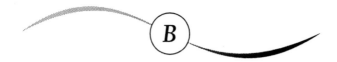

# Appendix

## Kabbalistic Meditation 1

### THE LIGHTNING FLASH, THE SERPENT'S PATH, AND THE MIDDLE PILLAR

To perform this meditation, it is necessary to know the three Hebrew letters known as the Three Fathers. They are Yod (י), He (ה), and Vav (ו). These three letters are permuted and used to seal the room in which the meditation takes place by directing various permutations of the three letters yod, he, and vav in six directions; up, down, forward (east), back (west), right side (south), left side (north).

This formula is given in *The Sepher Yetzirah*:

> He selected three letters from among the simple ones.
> And sealed them and formed them into a great name
> Yod He Vav
> And with this he sealed the universe in six directions.

I want everyone to close their eyes.

201

Sit up in the seat. Feet on the ground.

Now, we begin by doing some deep rhythmic breathing.

Start to a count of four.

Inhale, two, three, four.

Exhale, two, three, four.

Inhale, two, three, four. Exhale, two, three, four.

Inhale, two, three four. Exhale, two, three, four.

Inhale, two, three, four. Exhale, two, three, four. Continue like this for a while. Each count should be at least one second long.

Inhale, two, three, four. Exhale, two, three, four.

Try and keep this rhythm.

Imagine that you're looking upward even though your eyes are closed.

And you look above and you seal the highest heights with the letter Yod (י), with the letter Heh (ה), and with the letter Vav (ו).

You look below and you seal the depth with the letter Yod (י), Vav (ו), Heh (ה).

You look forward and seal it with Heh (ה), Yod (י), Vav (ו).

You look backward behind you and seal it with Heh (ה),

Vav (ו), Yod (י).

You look to the right and seal it with Vav (ו), Yod (י), Heh (ה).

You look to the left and seal it with Vav (ו), Heh (ה), Yod (י).

Now we've sealed this room or this space in six directions.

Using your imagination, push these six seals out to their furthest limits.

Above infinity and below infinity.

Before you and behind you out into infinity. To your right and to your left extend the seals out into infinity.

Now imagine above your head a triangle pointing upward, glowing, bright, getting brighter.

Picture this glowing triangle above your head and, from that triangle, there shoots down right into the top point of your crown like a lightning flash, a bolt of light coming from above to the top of your head.

Now, it moves from the top, which is Kether, to the right side of the head, which is Chokmah, to the left side of the head, which is Binah.

Now, it moves down through your throat and into your right shoulder, which is Chesed. Now, across your body to the left shoulder, which is Geburah. Now, down to the center of your chest, which is Tiphareth and then into the right hip, which is Netzach. Across into the left hip, which is Hod. Then, it moves into the genital area, Yesod. Then down to your feet. This is Malkuth.

Let it move down into your feet and actually through your feet and into the ground.

And below your feet is a downward pointing triangle.

Let the energy descend into that downward pointed triangle.

Hold it there for a moment and feel that the energy that you brought from above is grounded down into the earth so that we feel connected to the earth.

Now, slowly we can feel our energy want to rise up. Feel it as if it were bubbling under our feet, slowly wanting to move. Like a giant snake or giant serpent, it slowly rises up from that inverted triangle and moves up to the bottom of our feet—Malkuth.

It circles the bottom of the feet and slowly rises up our legs. It comes up to our genital area and slowly circles around our groin—Yesod. And moves slowly up to the left hip—Hod. It circles the left hip and moves across the body and circles the right hip—Netzach. Now, it moves upward to the center of the chest and circles around Tiphareth encompassing the area of our solar plexus and heart.

It then moves upward to the left shoulder, circles the left shoulder—Geburah.

It moves across the body and circles the right shoulder—Chesed. It moves up through the throat—Daath, and circles Daath.

Now, up to the left side of the head, the left side of the brain—Binah—circles Binah and moves to the right side of the brain and circles Chokmah.

It moves upward and circles around the highest point in the head—Kether.

Then it moves upward and continues up, up to the upward pointing triangle.

We've now gone through the Lightning Flash and the Serpent's Path.

Now, once again, we'll do the Lightning Flash, but faster this time.

So, again picture that upward pointing triangle floating above your head. See it gleaming, intensifying. Almost like a storm cloud ready to send out that Lightning Flash.

And—poof—it sends out the flash to the top of your skull. Now, to the right side of your head, to the left side. Down through your throat to your right shoulder. Across to your left shoulder, then down to the center of your chest. Now, down to the right hip, across to the left hip. Now, down to the genitals and down the legs into the feet. Ground it into the inverted triangle.

Let it rest there, grounded into the earth.

Now, once again we're going to let it rise, taking the Serpent's Path. Coming up slowly from the ground, circling the feet, moving slowly up the legs and circling the genital area.

Moving to the left side, circling there. Moving across the body to the right side, circling there. Moving up through the torso, circling around the center of the chest. To the left shoulder, circle. Across to the right shoulder, circle there. Up to the throat. It circles the throat. Up to the left side of the head. Circle.

To the right side of the head. Circle. Then up to the top of the crown and circle there. Then it slowly rises to the upward pointing triangle above your head.

Now, slowly. From this central triangle above your head, picture and feel the energy descend to a sphere about three inches in diameter at the top of your head. This sphere is Kether.

Picture Kether glowing. In the sphere of Kether, God's name is Eheieh (Eh-hey-yeh). I Am. Just feel as if the top of your head is floating. Floating along with the godhead, Kether.

Now, slowly feel the energy descend to our throats. Daath.

Picture a circle encompassing your throat. Inside the neck is a white, brilliantly glowing sphere of light. The God name of Daath is Yod He Vav He Elohim (El-oh-heem). Picture the sphere of knowledge and experience glowing inside your throat.

Now, the light descends once again to the center of the chest, in the area between the heart and the solar plexus. Right in the center of your chest. This is Tiphareth.

Picture this area glowing with a brilliant sphere of light in the center of your chest. The God name of Tiphareth is Yod He Vav He Eloah (El-oh-ah) Va Daath (Da-ath). See the light in the center of your chest.

Now, once again the light descends. Picture a glowing sphere encircling your genital area. Picture the light descending from Tiphareth to Yesod.

Feel yourself energized. Feel your life force energy increasing. The God name of Yesod is Shaddai (Shad-eye) El Chai (guttural sound like "ch" in loch and "eye" like the organ of sight). Feel the whole genital region alive with the light. The light of God.

Finally, the light descends one more time. Picture a sphere encompassing your feet and the light descends from Yesod down to Malkuth.

Picture a glowing sphere of light at your feet. The God name for Malkuth is Adonai (A-don-eye) Ha Aretz (Ah-rets).

We've now brought the light from above down through the Middle Pillar of Kether, Daath, Tiphareth, Yesod and Malkuth.

Now, bring the energy in your feet down to the downward pointed triangle below your feet.

Now, maintaining that downward pointing triangle, we take the Serpent's Path upward. To Malkuth, circle up to Yesod in the genital region. It circles Yesod and moves to the left hip. It circles Hod and moves across the body to the right hip—Netzach. It moves up to the center of the chest—Tiphareth. It circles and moves to the left shoulder. Circles and moves across the body to the right shoulder. It circles, then moves to the throat and circles, then moves up. Circles the left side of the head then moves across to the right side of the head and circles.

Now, picture it going upward to the top of the head and circling there.

Now, it continues to rise and enters the upward pointing triangle above your head.

Now, picture that upward pointing triangle.

We split our consciousness and are also aware of the downward pointing triangle below our feet.

The triangle above contains the energy of Heaven. The triangle below contains the energy of the Earth.

Now, from above, pull that upward pointing triangle down. Down into the top of your head. Through your head, through your throat and into the center of your chest.

So that now, in the center of your chest, you are visualizing an upward pointing triangle.

Now, direct your consciousness below and pull the downward pointed triangle upward. Through your feet, legs, genitals, abdomen and up to the center of the chest in Tiphareth.

The two triangles interlock and join.

You have the downward pointed triangle of the Earth, joining with the upward pointing triangle from Heaven. It is inside a sphere in the center of your chest. And it forms a six-pointed star. It unites the energy of Heaven and Earth.

For a minute or two, let's meditate on this heavenly and earthly energy combined inside of us now.

We begin to breathe rhythmically again.

Inhale, two, three, four.

Exhale, two, three, four.

Inhale, two, three, four.

Exhale, two, three, four.

Continue breathing slowly and rhythmically on your own.

Now, we let go and the upward pointed triangle and the downward pointed triangle separate.

The upward triangle rises through our body.

The downward pointed triangle descends through our body and enters the Earth.

The upward pointed triangle leaves our body and goes back to Heaven.

We dissolve any images in our head and in our body. We dissolve the sephiroth. Take a deep breath.

And let's slowly return to the room.

# Kabbalistic Meditation 2

## BUILDING THE TREE OF LIFE AND THE AURA

Begin by repeating the sealing of the Six Directions at the beginning of the Lightning Flash meditation using the Three Father Letters, Yod—He—Vav. Once the six directions are sealed and expanded into infinity, you begin breathing rhythmically.

Take a deep breath to the count of four.

Inhale, two, three, four.

Exhale, two, three, four.

Inhale, two, three, four.

Exhale, two, three, four.

Inhale, two, three, four.

Exhale, two, three, four.

Continue breathing rhythmically on your own.

Do the Lightning Flash and Serpent's Path and then the Middle Pillar down the center of the body as taught in previous Kaballistic Meditation. Do it at a rapid pace once you have mastered these techniques.

We pick up the meditation at the bottom of the Middle Pillar with our consciousness in Malkuth, visualizing and feeling a ball of light energy surrounding our feet.

From the bottom of your feet, feel a ball of energy that actually extends from the level of your ankles, encompassing your feet and actually extending into the ground, into the floor beneath your feet. Feel a ball of energy form there.

The ball rises up your legs, slowly to the level of your genitals into Yesod. It is the size of a small saucer, a saucer you would put a cup on. Feel the ball of energy at your sexual organs.

Use your mind and your will power to move the ball of energy.

Now, let the ball of energy rise up to the center of your chest at the solar plexus-heart level of Tiphareth. Picture and feel the ball of energy growing brighter and stronger, taking on a more concrete form. Take that sphere and push it back toward your backbone. As you do that, you feel a tingling rush of energy going toward your head. Going upward.

This glowing ball of energy rises to the throat, the level of Daath. See and feel it encompass the entire neck and throat from the bottom of your chin to where your neck connects with your chest.

Now, the ball of energy rises again all the way to the top of the skull. Picture and feel it as a ball of glowing light floating halfway within and halfway above the top of your head. This is Kether.

We've now run the Middle Pillar both down and up the center of the body.

From the top sephirah, from Kether, feel a shaft of energy move downward to the right side of your head. Feel a ball of energy form at the right side of your head that seems to extend from your right eyeball out past your ear. This is Chokmah.

Return to Kether and feel the energy go out to the left side of your head. Form a ball of energy from your left eyeball out past your ear. This is Binah.

Feel the three sephiroth connect. Feel a line go from Kether to Chokmah. From Chokmah across the middle of your skull to Binah. Feel the energy travel back and forth. Then, from Binah up to Kether go back and forth. You can feel a triangle form. A mental triangle connecting Kether, Chokmah, and Binah.

Now, from Chokmah on the right, feel the energy descend down to the level of the right shoulder. Feel a ball of energy form at your right shoulder. This is Chesed.

Similarly, on your left side, descending from Binah to your left shoulder, form a ball of energy at Geburah.

Now, connect the sephiroth. Feel the energy travel from Chokmah at the level of your right eye down to your right shoulder, then across the upper portion of your chest. From Chesed to Geburah at your left shoulder, feel the energy go back and forth from the left side to the right side, from the right side to the left side. Actually feel energy moving across the body. Now, connect Chokmah, Binah, Chesed, and Geburah and you feel a great rectangle of force from Chokmah down to Chesed across to Geburah and up to Binah at the level of your left eye. And across to Chokmah. You should feel this very strongly now.

Go back to your right shoulder. Now, feel the energy descend into Tiphareth which is a sphere at the level encompassing the heart and the solar plexus in the center of the chest.

Similarly, from the left shoulder, feel the energy descend into Tiphareth so that we form a triangle that encompasses your left shoulder and your right shoulder and the center of your chest. Feel the energy circulate from your right shoulder to Tiphareth in the center of your chest, up to your left shoulder, then across your body. Feel that triangle.

You can now begin to really feel this energy body taking shape within you.

Now, from your right shoulder, you feel the energy go down the right side of your body all the way to your right hip. Form a ball of energy in your right hip. This is Netzach. Feel the energy at the right hip. Form a ball there. Feel it grow brighter.

Similarly, on the left side, feel the energy descend from your left shoulder down to your left hip where you feel a ball of energy form there. This is Hod. Now, connect the left hip, Netzach, with the right hip, Hod. The whole area of your chest, torso and abdomen forms a large rectangle of energy.

Now, return to Tiphareth in the center of your chest. You already can feel the energy from your right shoulder and left shoulder descend into Tiphareth. And now from Tiphareth, feel the energy descend on the right side into your right hip. You can feel that connection.

From Tiphareth, again feel the energy descend on the left side into Hod. And feel this giant triangle in your body. From Tiphareth to Netzach then across the body at the level of your hip into your left hip at Hod. Go back and forth and establish the energy there. Then from the left hip up to the center of your chest.

Feel the energy in your right hand. This is also Netzach. Move energy from your right shoulder to your right hand—from Chesed to Netzach.

Feel the energy in your left hand. This is also Hod. Send energy from the left shoulder to your left hand—from Geburah to Hod.

Now, from your right hip, feel the energy descend to Yesod at the sexual organs. Feel a ball of energy form there.

Similarly, from the left hip, feel the energy descend from Hod to Yesod. From the left hip to your sexual organ. So, here we have a small triangle connecting both hips and the sexual organs. Feel the energy circulating there.

Now, from your right hip, feel the energy descend all the way down to your foot. Feel the energy go back and forth, up and down the right leg and into your right foot.

From the left side, from Hod, feel the energy go down your left leg, down to Malkuth in your left foot. Move it up and down. Feel that energy connect with your right foot, form a ball of energy in both feet, it moves up the right leg to Netzach, then across the hips to Hod. This forms a large triangle.

Now, we have connected all the sephiroth and created all the intersecting paths.

Now, again bring your awareness to the top of your skull and begin to move the energy down the left side of your body. All the way down. Down the side of your head, past your shoulder, down your arm and the left side of your body. Down your left leg. Down to your left foot. Then have it move into your right foot and it begins to travel up the right side. Up the right leg past the right hip, up the right arm and side of the body, up to the right shoulder, past the right ear and back to the top of the head.

You can synchronize the movement with your breath. As you exhale, the energy goes down the left side of your body. As you inhale, two, three, four, the energy goes up the right side of your body.

Exhale, two, three, four and the energy moves down.

Inhale, two, three, four and the energy moves up.

Continue circulating the energy around the sides of your body.

Now, again move your point of concentration to the top of your head. We will now circulate the energy down the front of the body to the feet and then up the back of the body to the top of the head.

Down past the face, throat, chest, hips, legs, feet. Then,

up the back of the calves, thighs, buttocks, back, neck to the top of the head.

Exhale and the energy goes down the front of the body, two, three, four.

Inhale, two, three, four and the energy goes up the back.

Continue doing this. Down, two, three, four. Up, two, three, four.

Now, put your awareness on your feet. And as you inhale feel the energy that we have created seem to come right up through the soles of our feet and travel up our body. Travel up the Middle Pillar. As we inhale, it goes all the way up to the top of our head. And as we exhale, the energy spews out of the top of our head like a shower all around us. 360 degrees. Forming an egg-like aura around us. As we inhale, two, three, four, the energy is absorbed through the soles of our feet and travels up the Middle Pillar and when we exhale, two, three, four, the energy showers out of the top of our head.

Inhale, two, three, four. The energy is absorbed up.

Exhale, two, three, four. The energy sprays out above and descends all around us.

We have built an aura, a mental aura around our body.

Continue drawing the energy up through your feet and out the top of your head.

A connected system. Nothing is wasted. Nothing is lost. The energy circulates as bright light.

Bring your concentration back to the top of your head. To Kether. Feel that ball of energy at the top of your head. Slowly feel that ball of energy at the top of your head loosen itself from your skull and start to rise up. It rises up slowly. It is no longer in your body, but is outside your body where you're now touching the next level. We are now touching the level of Yetzirah.

And you may sense another whole Tree of Life above you. But for now, you will explore no further. But, next time you do this on your own, you may go higher and form the sphere above, you may form another sphere and another sphere until you have formed a whole Tree outside yourself and circulate the energy through all the paths above you.

But for now, let's collect the energy. Slowly feel the energy dropping back down into our body, down from our head and slowly move toward the ground and into our feet.

Put your awareness on your feet. Feel you are connected to the ground you stand on and the earth below you.

Breathe deeply, two, three, four and feel this ball of energy dissolve.

Breathe deeply, two, three, four and feel yourself return to the room.

At your own pace, open your eyes and come back. Take a deep breath and feel that you are fully back to the real world of Malkuth.

# Kabbalistic Meditation 3

## THE THREE MOTHER LETTERS MEDITATION

Begin by Sealing the Six Directions.

Close your eyes.

Begin breathing rhythmically to the count of four.

Inhale, two, three, four.

Exhale, two, three, four.

Inhale, two, three, four.

Exhale, two, three, four.

Inhale, two, three, four.

Exhale, two, three, four.

Continue breathing deeply and rhythmically on your own.

Picture yourself outside on a beautiful sunny day. The sun is bright overhead and warms your forehead and the hair on your head. It feels good. So bright and warm. It fills your whole head with heat. You can feel the heat radiating. You can see the light of the sun in your whole head. Lighting it up.

Continue breathing rhythmically as you do this. Remember you're standing outside on a beautiful, sunny, warm day. It's a bright sky with the sun up above as if it were created just for you. Picture in your head the letter Shin (ש). It looks like a "W". It's sound is Sh-h-h-h. It is the Mother Letter of fire. Fire is the energy that brought forth the sun. The sun is just a local expression of the power of the Shin.

Whenever you want to bring forth the fire energy, just picture the letter Shin (ש) in your head.

Continue to stand outside on this beautiful day. It's as if the sun is in your head. As if you are the sun. Radiating.

Breathe rhythmically. Inhale, two, three, four. Exhale, two, three, four and make the sound Sh-h-h-h. Inhale, two, three, four. Exhale, two, three, four, Sh-h-h-h. As you continue to breath like this, you notice a strange thing happening. It's as if the air itself is coming right through the skin of your body and into your chest.

Picture yourself. You're standing outside in the same place as you were before. Under a clear blue sky. It's a warm sun up above, but the air has a sort of crispness to it. And as you inhale, you can feel the air coming right into your chest. Coming through the skin in front of your body, in the back of your body, right through the skin of your arms and armpits, left and right side.

How delightful. It's as if you no longer even need your lungs. The air penetrates right into your body. And as you exhale, you exhale right through the skin of your body. And it feels as if there were a different type of skin on your body. Something rubbery and elastic yet porous at the same time. And when you really think about it and put your concentration there, the air seems to go right through the skin and penetrate into the flesh and bones of your whole body.

Continue breathing rhythmically. Inhale, two, three, four and the air passes right through your skin. Exhale, two, three, four and the air passes out from the bones and flesh below the skin.

Inhale, two, three, four.

Exhale, two, three, four.

Picture the letter Aleph (א) in your chest. Aleph is the letter that sounds like Ah-h-h-h. Silently, to yourself, picture the letter Aleph and make the sound Ah-h-h-h. Feel the air going right through your body.

Continue to breathe rhythmically. Inhale, two, three, four. Exhale the air right through your skin. Ah-h-h-h. Inhale, two, three, four. Exhale Ah-h-h-h.

How delightful a feeling, as if we are floating on air. And our body seems to grow lighter and less weighty. And we can just float around.

Continue floating as you breath rhythmically.

And you realize that you're still standing out there although it feels as if you're floating. And the sun is overhead and the Shin is in your head, and the Aleph is in your chest.

And you suddenly become aware that you are standing in a beautiful pool of water. It's been there all this time but you weren't even aware of it until now.

You're in a pool. And the water comes right up over your hands which are by your sides up to the tops of your wrists. And up to the level of your navel, covering your lower abdomen.

That water is cool. And it feels good. And the whole lower half of your body feels cool. And you can feel that coolness coming in through the tips of your fingers. And as you continue to breath in rhythmically, you feel the coolness coming right into the tips of your toes. Right into your toes and up your legs and your thighs and your buttocks and sexual organs. A coolness in your belly right up to your navel. Cool.

M-m-m-m-m-m. That feels good. Picture the letter Mem (מ). Picture it inside your body hanging just below your navel. Make the sound M-m-m-m-m and feel that coolness down there.

Breathe in rhythmically and feel that cool water coming right through your body. Right up the tips of your fingers and up the tips of your toes. And through your skin.

Inhale, two, three, four.

Exhale M-m-m-m-m.

Inhale, two, three, four.

Exhale M-m-m-m-m.

And you're standing in this pool of water. A beautiful pool. Look in front of you. You can see that you're standing in a pool. You can see the sides of the pool. It's long and rectangular.

Beyond the pool you can see trees. And the sky is crystal blue above you. Ah-h-h-h. The air is coming right into your chest and right through your skin. It feels good. Inhale, two, three, four. Exhale Ah-h-h-h.

The fiery sun above. Sh-h-h-h. Inhale, two, three, four. Exhale Sh-h-h-h.

Picture the Aleph in your chest. Let it sink to the lowest point in the chest. Let it sink all the way down to the level of the solar plexus.

Right at the level of your solar plexus you can see the letter Aleph inside your body. The Aleph is the ancient Hebrew letter for our letter "A". Inhale, two, three, four. Exhale Ah-h-h-h.

Now feel the heat in your head. The fiery heat encompassing your head slowly sinks down. The Shin, which looks like a "W," sinks down to the top of Aleph. All the way down to your solar plexus. Picture the Shin sitting on top of the Aleph.

From below, feel the coolness of the water and picture the letter Mem. See the letter Mem slowly float to the top of the water. Right to the bottom of the Aleph. You feel a joining of the three letters. The Mem, the Aleph, and the Shin at your solar plexus. The fire of Shin sits on the Aleph of air and the Mem of water sits below the Aleph of air. The Mem supports the Aleph and the Shin.

Now, picture both the Shin, the fire above, and the Mem of water from below, move right into the Aleph of air as if they were being absorbed. And in that one place you feel the joining of the heat and the cool and the mediating air and feel them mix there. Feel them mix so that you have coolness and heat, dryness and moistness mixing around. Feel them all slowly neutralize. Feel the different elements mix and neutralize into a homogenous blend.

Now, feel it begin to spin. So that it appears that there is just a jumble of letters, the Aleph, the Mem and the Shin, spinning around forming a circle, forming a sphere, forming a sephirah in the very center of your body. Now, let the spin continue rapidly in a clockwise direction.

Now, slowly stop and reverse the direction of the spin. Let it spin around.

Now stop. Just let your mind concentrate on the joining of the Shin, Mem and Aleph. Fire, water and air in the center of your body. And breathe rhythmically.

Inhale, two, three, four.

Exhale, two, three, four.

Inhale, two, three, four.

Exhale, two, three, four.

The letters begin to move back to their proper place. The Mem moves below, down to the lower abdomen. The Shin separates and moves up toward your head. The Aleph remains in your chest.

The Shin moves back up to your head. The Aleph, the air, dissolves in your chest and you breath regularly. And the Mem, the cold water, moves down to your lower abdomen. Make the Healing Sound for the Three Mothers, Sh-h-h-h-ah-h-h-h-m-m-m-m.

Sound out the letter Zain (z). Z-z-z-z-z. The energy shoots down your leg like a jolt of lightning. It grounds you deep into the Earth. Down below your feet, past the base of the pool. You feel grounded and attached to the earth. To the Kabbalist, water is the source of the Earth element.

Slowly continue to breathe regularly. And when you feel ready, open your eyes and come back to the room.

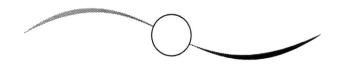

# Bibliography

Bardon, Franz. *Initiation into Hermetics*. Dieter Ruggeberg, 1956.

———. *The Key to the True Quabbalah*. Dieter Ruggeberg, 1957.

Blofeld, John. *Taoist Mysteries and Magic*. Shambalah, 1973.

Burnham, Robert Jr. *Burnham's Celestial Handbook*. Dover Publications Inc., 1978.

Castenada, Carlos. *Tales of Power*. Simon and Schuster, 1974.

Chia, Mantak. *Awaken Healing Energy Through the Tao*. Aurora Press, 1983.

———, with Michael Wynn. *Taoist Secrets of Love: Cultivating Male Sexual Energy*. Aurora Press, 1984.

————. *Taoist Ways to Transform Stress into Vitality*. Healing Tao Press, 1985.

————. *Chi-Self Massage*. Healing Tao Press, 1986.

————. with Maneewan Chia. *Healing Love Through the Tao: Cultivating Female Sexual Energy*. Healing Tao Press, 1986.

————. *Iron Shirt Chi Kung*. Healing Tao Press, 1986.

————. *Bone Marrow Nei Kung*. Healing Tao Press, 1988.

————. *Fusion of the Five Elements I*. Healing Tao Press, 1989.

————. *Chi Nei Tsang Internal Organs Massage*. Healing Tao Press, 1990.

————. *Awaken Healing Light of the Tao*. Healing Tao Press, 1993.

Cleary, Thomas. *The Secret of the Golden Flower*. Harper Collins, 1991.

Crowley, Aleister. *Atlantis*. Dove Press, undated.

————. *The Book of The Law*. Samual Weiser, 1976.

————. *The Book of Thoth*. Lancer Books, undated.

————. *The Equinox*. Reprinted Samuel Weiser, 1972.

————. *Magick in Theory and Practice*. Castle Books, undated.

————. *777*. Samuel Weiser, 1970.

Culling, Louis T. *A Manual of Sex Magick*. Llewellyn Press, 1971.

Epstein, Perle. *Kabbalah the Way of the Jewish Mystic*. Shambala Publications, 1978.

Frater U.D. *Secrets of the German Sex Magicians*. Llewellyn Publications, 1991.

Hawking, Stephen. *A Brief History of Time*. Bantam Books, 1988.

Ishihara, Akira, and Howard Levy. *The Tao of Sex*. Shibundo, 1968.

Kalisch, Dr.Isidore. *Sepher Yetzirah*. L.H. Frank, 1877.

Kaplan, Aryeh. *Meditation and Kabbalah*. Samuel Weiser, 1982.

————. *Jewish Meditation*. Schoken Books, 1985.

————. *Sefer Yetzirah*. Samuel Weiser, 1990.

King, Francis. *The Western Tradition of Magic*. Avon, 1975.

De Leon, Moses (Simeon Ben Yohai). *The Zohar*. Numerous editions and translations.

Luk, Charles (Lu K'uan Yu). *The Secrets of Chinese Meditation*. Samuel Weiser, 1969.

————. *Taoist Yoga*. Samuel Weiser, 1973.

Ponce, Charles. *Kabbalah*. Straight Arrow Books, 1973.

Reuchlin, Johann. *On the Art of the Kabbalah*. University of Nebraska Press, 1993.

Richardson, Alan. *An Introduction to the Mystical Qabalah*. Samuel Weiser, 1974.

Regardie, Israel. *The Golden Dawn*. Llewellyn Publications, 1937.

————. *The One Year Manual*. Samuel Weiser, 1981.

Scholem, Gershom. *Kabbalah*. Keter Publishing House, 1974.

————. *Modern Trends in Jewish Mysticism*. Schocken Books, 1961.

Torrens, R.G. *The Secret Rituals of the Golden Dawn*. Samuel Weiser, 1973.

Waite, A.E. *The Holy Kabbalah*. Citidel Press, 1990.

Ware, James R. (Translator). *Alchemy, Medicine and Religion in the China of 320 A.D.: The Nei Pien of Ko Hung*. Dover Publications, 1966.

Westcott, W. Wynn. *Sepher Yetzirah or Book of Formation*. 1893.

Wilhelm, Richard. *The I Ching*. Princeton University Press, 1950.

————. *The Secret of the Golden Flower*. Harvest Books, 1931.

∽

# Index

# Stay in Touch. . .

**Llewellyn publishes hundreds of books
on your favorite subjects**

On the following pages you will find listed some books now available on related subjects. Your local bookstore stocks most of these and will stock new Llewellyn titles as they become available. We urge your patronage.

## Order by Phone

Call toll-free within the U.S. and Canada, 1–800–THE MOON.
In Minnesota call (612) 291–1970.
We accept Visa, MasterCard, and American Express.

## Order by Mail

Send the full price of your order (MN residents add 7% sales tax) in U.S. funds to:

> Llewellyn Worldwide
> P.O. Box 64383, Dept. K250X
> St. Paul, MN 55164–0383, U.S.A.

## Postage and Handling

- ◆ $4.00 for orders $15.00 and under
- ◆ $5.00 for orders over $15.00
- ◆ No charge for orders over $100.00

We ship UPS in the continental United States. We cannot ship to P.O. boxes. Orders shipped to Alaska, Hawaii, Canada, Mexico, and Puerto Rico will be sent first-class mail.

International orders: Airmail—add freight equal to price of each book to the total price of order, plus $5.00 for each non-book item (audiotapes, etc.). Surface mail—Add $1.00 per item.

Allow 4–6 weeks delivery on all orders. Postage and handling rates subject to change.

## Group Discounts

We offer a 20% quantity discount to group leaders or agents. You must order a minimum of 5 copies of the same book to get our special quantity price.

## Free Catalog

Get a free copy of our color catalog, *New Worlds of Mind and Spirit*. Subscribe for just $10.00 in the United States and Canada ($20.00 overseas, first class mail). Many bookstores carry *New Worlds*—ask for it!

All prices subject to change without notice

## ECSTASY THROUGH TANTRA

### by Dr. Jonn Mumford

Dr. Jonn Mumford makes the occult dimension of the sexual dynamic accessible to everyone. One need not go up to the mountaintop to commune with Divinity: its temple is the body, its sacrament the communion between lovers. *Ecstasy Through Tantra* traces the ancient practices of sex magick through the Egyptian, Greek and Hebrew forms, where the sexual act is viewed as symbolic of the highest union, to the highest expression of Western sex magick.

Dr. Mumford guides the reader through mental and physical exercises aimed at developing psychosexual power; he details the various sexual practices and positions that facilitate "psychic short-circuiting" and the arousal of Kundalini, the Goddess of Life within the body. He shows the fundamental unity of Tantra with Western Wicca, and he plumbs the depths of Western sex magick, showing how its techniques culminate in spiritual illumination. Includes 14 full-color photographs.

**0-87542-494-5, 190 pgs., 6 x 9, 14 color plates, softcover**
**$16.00**

# BETWEEN THE WORLDS
## WITCHCRAFT & THE TREE OF LIFE: A PROGRAM OF SPIRITUAL DEVELOPMENT

### by Stuart Myers

Witches, pagans and Goddess worshippers in general will find *Between the Worlds* a must-have guide to spiritual development in the Wiccan Tradition. But this workbook also will be of interest to Qabalists with its new, thought-provoking overview of a Goddess-oriented Qabalah!

Through a blend of science, philosophy and brilliant ritual, *Between the Worlds* provides instruction in Qabalistic Witchcraft and all phases of Wicca in conjunction with the Tree of Life. Learn invocations and rituals in both a Qabalistic and Wiccan framework through step-by-step instruction. Students will find all the basics of the Old Religion explored, and even the newcomer to Wicca and Qabalah will find it easy to use the material. This complete system of Qabalistic Witchcraft includes explanations, diagrams, charts, illustrations and appendixes for easier learning.

1-56718-480-4, 256 pgs., 7 x 10, illus., softcover

$17.95

## MOVING WITH THE WIND
### MAGICK AND HEALING
### IN THE MARTIAL ARTS

### Brian Crowley with Esther Crowley

Tap into the incredible and mysterious force that can empower you to attain perfect mental control and spiritual enlightenment, perform bodily healing through invisible means, live a prolonged and vigorous life... or even cut a pile of bricks in half with a bare fist. This mysterious power is the fundamental secret that lies at the foundation of all esoteric systems. It is the control of pranic energies, of the force known simply as "chi," which is said to permeate and motivate all things throughout the universe.

Against a backdrop that traces the spiritual philosophy, history and development of major martial art forms, *Moving with the Wind* explores the origin and nature of this intrinsic but still occult and magickal (to Western science at least) chi force that underlies all the oriental fighting forms—and offers a set of easy-to-follow exercises—with special emphasis on the healing arts sometimes associated with martial arts activity—that will help you develop your own chi reservoir for practical daily use, or to prepare yourself for martial arts training.

0-87542-134-2, 192 pgs., 5 1/4 x 8, illus., softcover
$10.00